SpringerBriefs in Criminology

Policing

*Series Editor*

M. R. Haberfeld, John Jay College of Criminal Justice (CUNY)
New York, NY, USA

For further volumes:
http://www.springer.com/series/11179

Jon Shane

# Learning from Error in Policing

A Case Study in Organizational
Accident Theory

 Springer

Jon Shane
Department of Law, Police Science
 and Criminal Justice Administration
John Jay College of Criminal Justice
New York, NY
USA

ISSN 2194-6213          ISSN 2194-6221   (electronic)
ISBN 978-3-319-00040-4   ISBN 978-3-319-00041-1   (eBook)
DOI 10.1007/978-3-319-00041-1
Springer Heidelberg New York Dordrecht London

Library of Congress Control Number: 2013932560

Printed on acid-free paper

Springer is part of Springer Science+Business Media (www.springer.com)

# Foreword

When a commercial aircraft crashes, no one doubts that a significant failure has occurred. Steps are quickly taken to identify the sources of error in order to learn from the tragedy and prevent future mishaps. So, too, when a patient dies at a teaching hospital, doctors convene morbidity and mortality conferences to study the case and identify lessons that may prevent further mishaps. Yet, when the criminal justice system makes an error by wrongly convicting an innocent person, the case typically gets much less attention. In the United States, police and prosecutors rarely call for an inquiry or convene a panel of their peers to sift through the mistakes that may have led to the erroneous conviction. It is as if the professionals we charge with securing our safety are unwilling to acknowledge that they make mistakes and are uninterested in improving their work.

The situation is even worse when the innocent suspect is "merely" indicted, but not convicted. Here, we can say that the system "worked" on some level by dismissing the case prior to conviction. But we are still left with questions about why the police would arrest an innocent person and why prosecutors would push to indict and begin to pursue a case against someone who did not commit the crime.

I do not begrudge police and prosecutors for making mistakes. That is the natural consequence of any system that is built on human processes and decision making. Planes unfortunately crash; patients occasionally die in surgery; and innocent suspects are sometimes indicted and less often convicted of crimes they did not commit. But, unless the criminal justice system is willing to investigate its errors, we are all in a poor position to prevent those mistakes.

If police and prosecutors were to join forces to analyze erroneous convictions, they would likely learn that the sources of error are multifaceted and interlocking. Rarely is there one mistake that "causes" an erroneous indictment or conviction. Even when an eyewitness identifies the wrong suspect, a prosecution can often be avoided if relevant forensic evidence is properly collected and tested or the suspect is represented by a capable and zealous advocate. Nor does police or prosecution error likely exist in a vacuum. The officer that unintentionally offers feedback to a witness during a show-up was likely trained by a department that is not up to date on best practices or does not follow up with adequate supervision. The prosecutor who does not appreciate a witness' ulterior motives in lying may lack mentoring from more experienced lawyers who have encountered similar situations in the past.

It is the organizational context of these errors that makes them so ripe for investigation and so promising for correction. Fortunately, we now have Jon Shane's compelling inquiry into organizational failure. In the book that follows, he applies a systems theory of causation to the existence of an erroneous indictment. Distinguishing between latent conditions, organizational factors, and both active and passive failures, Dr. Shane makes a significant contribution to our understanding of how errors occur in the criminal justice system. Rather than weeding out "bad apples" or correcting single policies, his work shows us that efforts are needed at several levels within criminal justice institutions and among multiple categories of professionals to prevent wrongful convictions and mistaken indictments. Is the process of identifying and rectifying mistakes likely to be easy? No. But, as Dr. Shane clearly illustrates, the consequences are too significant to ignore.

Jon B. Gould

Jon Gould is professor and director of the Washington Institute for Public and International Affairs Research at American University, where he also teaches at the Washington College of Law. He has published extensively on erroneous convictions. He is author of *The Innocence Commission: Preventing Wrongful Convictions and Restoring the Criminal Justice System* (NYU Press 2007) and is the lead author of a research project funded by the U.S. National Institute of Justice titled *Predicting Erroneous Convictions: A Social Science Approach to Miscarriages of Justice*.

# Acknowledgments

The author thanks Maki Haberfeld, Ph.D., John Jay College for her comments and assistance; James Doyle, J. D. and Jon Gould, Ph.D. for their insight and contribution; Nicky Miller, Ph.D., and Julia Morris, National Policing Improvement Agency (U.K.) for facilitating the research; the participating attorneys who made the case available; and the anonymous reviewers who made this better.

# Contents

# Abstract

This study explores an organizational accident that occurred in American policing, but the context and circumstances have direct implications for all rule-of-law societies that practice democratic law enforcement. While the proximate cause of any accident is usually someone's immediate action or omission, there is often a trail of underlying latent conditions that facilitated the error; the person has, in effect, been unwittingly "set up" for failure by the organization. The study is described in terms of organizational accident theory, which suggests a single unsafe act—in this case a wrongful arrest—is facilitated by several underlying latent conditions that triggered the event and failed to stop the harm once it was set in motion. The analyses show the risk of errors committed by omission were significantly more likely to occur than errors committed by acts of commission and among them, procedural omissions posed the greatest risk. The analysis also reveals proof of concept for the organizational accident model. Policy implications and directions for future research are discussed.

**Keywords** Organizational accident · Learning from error · Eyewitness · Show-up · Near miss · Police · Robbery investigation · Case study · Probable cause · Wrongful arrest

# Chapter 1
# Introduction

Learning from error has been explored in other industries, most notably medicine,[1] aeronautics and transportation,[2] petroleum and nuclear production,[3] and business.[4] When Tom Watson Jr., chief executive officer of IBM in the 1960s, summoned a subordinate executive to his office to answer for losing $10 million in a recent venture, the junior executive feared termination was certain. Watson remarked "Fire you? I spent $10 million educating you. I just want to be sure you learned the right lessons."[5] Criminal justice is a discipline that is not as forgiving…and policing in particular, which is at the sharp end[6] of the criminal justice process is often the source of errors and failures whose origins can be traced to initial and follow-up investigative activities such as relying on coerced confessions, flawed eyewitness identification processes, and shoddy investigations that fail to corroborate facts and uncover supporting evidence.[7]

How the police behave as a given case unfolds determines whether the criminal justice apparatus is activated to meet the impending challenge. As the gatekeepers

---

[1] Leape [1]; Wu et al. [2]; Meurier et al. [3]; Kohn et al. [4]; Lawton and Parker [5]; Armitage [6].

[2] Starbuck and Farjoun [7]; Vaughan [8]; Hall [9]; Birkland [10]; National Transportation Safety Board, Railroad Accident Report–Derailment Of Chicago Transit Authority Train Number 220 Between Clark/Lake and Grand/Milwaukee Stations, (Chicago, IL July 11, 2006); National Transportation Safety Board, Collision of Two Washington Metropolitan Area Transit Authority Metrorail Trains Near Fort Totten Station (Washington, D.C. June 22, 2009).

[3] Deep Water Horizon Study Group [11]; Neshkati [12]; Furuta et al. [13].

[4] Homsma et al. [14].

[5] Paul B. Carroll & Chunka Mui, *Failed Strategies: What CEOs Can Learn From The Billion Dollar Mistakes of Others,* The Chief Executive (Sept–Oct 2008).

[6] The "sharp end" of a system is the point of execution, where the failure has an immediate impact resulting from an overt act or omission. Contrast this against the "blunt end" of the system, which is the point of system design, where the failure has a lagging impact from dormant or inchoate conditions.

[7] Scheck et al. [15]; Garrett [16]; Ede and Shephard [17]; Leo [18]; Kassin et al. [19]; Gould and Leo [20]; Steblay et al. [21]; Yarmey et al. [22]; Connors et al. [23]; Kassin [24]; PBS Frontline, *The Confessions* (documenting the trial of four men who falsely confessed to a murder in Norfolk, VA that they did not commit; the confessions were based largely on oppressive, yet legal police tactics that are tantamount to failure in a police organization, *see* [25]. Accessible at http://www.pbs.org/wgbh/pages/frontline/the-confessions, 2010).

J. Shane, *Learning from Error in Policing*, SpringerBriefs in Policing,
DOI: 10.1007/978-3-319-00041-1_1, © The Author(s) 2013

of the criminal justice system,[8] free societies rely on competent, technically proficient police officers who execute their duties according to the rule of law. It is in this realm that democratic policing is carried out, hopefully with a deep appreciation from the officers that their actions serve to both protect the innocent and call the accused to account as they sift through the facts to ferret out the truth.[9]

When the police make mistakes, the proximate cause is often traced to one or more active failures supported by one or more latent conditions that align in time and space to produce harmful results, such as an unlawful arrest, unlawful search, personal injury, or death. When searching for the causes of the harm, it is not sufficient to examine the active failure in isolation from the organizational context in which it occurred, which means also examining the cascade of underlying conditions that coexisted and perhaps facilitated the unsafe acts. While the individual operator is not absolved from responsibility for their acts or omissions, they are operating inside a bureaucracy that has ensnared them with a set of cultural and operating practices that may deviate from accepted standards; this suggests the employee "inherits" rather than "instigates" the accident sequence.

Correcting system (i.e., organizational) failures requires a systems approach, except the traditional—and typically cathartic—approach in policing's culture of blame is to find the guilty *individual*, then undergo a disciplinary ritual and enact more rules or laws to tighten control. Internal police investigations often move directly to affixing blame and forego examining the context in which the officer is situated, which is partly due to the strict liability nature of police rules and regulations that are not concerned with why a rule was violated, only that it was. Society often assumes that individual decisions are the product of human agency or free will; in reality, even the best decisions are constrained by organizational policies, personal preparedness and situational circumstances beyond the individual's control. So, punishing the individual has limited impact, although there are legal and technical reasons to do so; there is symbolic value in individual punishment, but that does little to correct the underlying problem, shape a culture of safety and develop organizational learning and personal mastery. Inevitably, the system in which the individual resides is still the same with enduring endemic issues.[10] A systems approach to reducing error implies that in response to those errors, the focus for corrective action must be how the established organizational policies and processes (latent conditions) contributed to the individual's actions (active failures) that triggered the event. This approach begins from the premise that: (1) active failures have their origins in organizational processes and arise from a combination of several contributing factors originating at different levels of the organization; (2) individual factors may seem relatively innocuous in isolation, but taken together can create a unique combination of failures that creates an

---

[8]  Bryett et al. [26]; Friedrich [27]; Gottfredson and Gottfredson [28]; Konecni and Ebbesen [29].
[9]  Packer [30].
[10]  Sagan [31]; Doyle [32].

opportunity for an "organizational accident"[11]; and (3) in this context, focusing on the individual is a necessary but insufficient response to preventing future accidents, because such an approach does little to address the wider systemic failures that may have contributed to the error.[12] From such an approach is likely to flow a culture of safety that protects citizens and police officers alike from the harms inflicted by errors in the criminal justice process.[13]

Learning from error is a neglected area of criminal justice research generally and police management research specifically. This study explores how an organizational accident may occur in policing by examining a single case. From this case, some general propositions about police practices are constructed by following the path of inductive reasoning, where the individual failure points during the investigation are explored, which lead to risk estimates. The interest here is in patterns of repeated behavior observed across different police officers in a single event so inferences may be drawn about factors that contribute to those patterns, specifically how and why the behavior occurs.

This case involves a "show-up"[14] identification procedure that was executed during a robbery investigation of a retail store conducted by a municipal police department. The same municipal police department then conducted a follow-up investigation along with the County prosecutor's office. A show-up procedure is inherently suggestive and may be prone to errors. This case relied exclusively upon the victim's equivocal identification and the police failed to collect any corroborating evidence. Although this case involves an armed robbery, it is easily substituted for a vehicular pursuit, an officer-involved shooting, an in-custody death, an improperly executed search warrant, or any other risky police enforcement function that may result in harmful consequences.

This case offers a rare glimpse inside police practice as it is carried out in the field since organizational accidents in police work are rarely, if ever, officially reported or investigated, which unfortunately keeps their learning value away from the broader policing community. The analysis is drawn from a civil lawsuit against the local police department and the County prosecutor's office following the plaintiff's wrongful arrest for robbery. Ultimately, the case against the three alleged offenders was never prosecuted, the indictment was dismissed, no new evidence was uncovered, no new arrests were made and the investigation remains

---

[11]  Reason [33]; Reason [34].

[12]  Charles Perrow, Normal Accidents 9 (1984) (an accident is termed "normal" when an individual properly observes all established standards); Vincent and Bark [35].

[13]  Doyle [36].

[14]  A show-up is "A direct one-on-one examination of the actual person, place or object previously described within a reasonable period of time and within a reasonable distance from the crime scene for the purposes of confirming or dispelling suspicion that the alleged person, place or object was involved in the crime" (see Holtz [37]; also see U.S. Department of Justice [38]; State v. Dubose, 699 N.W.2d 582, 584 n.1 (Wis. 2005) ("A 'show-up' is an out-of-court pretrial identification procedure in which a suspect is presented singly to a witness for identification purposes.").

closed; the resulting civil lawsuit was settled. The findings suggest that the initial response, the follow-up investigation, and the supervision in this case were flawed in ways that indicate a disregard for reasonable and accepted practice standards and judgment, which implies that the accident may have been preventable.

# References

1. Leape, L. L. (1994). Error in medicine. *Journal of the American Medical Association, 272,* 1851–1857.
2. Wu, A.W., Folkman, S., McPbee, S. J., & Lo, B. (1991). Do house officers learn from their mistakes? *Journal of the American Medical Association, 265,* 2089–2094.
3. Meurier, G. E., Vincent, G. A., & Parmar, D. G., (1997). Learning from errors in nursing practice. *Journal of Advanced Nursing, 26,* 111–119.
4. Kohn, L. T., Corrigan, J. M., & Donaldson, M. S. (Eds.). (2000). *To err is human: Building a safer health system.* Washington, D.C.: National Academy Press.
5. Lawton, R. & Parker, D. (2002). Barriers to incident reporting in a healthcare system, II. *Quality and Safety Health Care, 15,* 15–18.
6. Armitage, G. (2009). Human error theory: Relevance to nurse management. *Journal of Nursing Management, 17,* 193–202.
7. Starbuck, W. H., & Farjoun, M. (Eds.). (2005) Organization at the limit: Lessons from the Columbia disaster. Malden, MA: Blackwell Scientific.
8. Vaughan, D. (1996). *The challenger launch decision: Risky technology, culture and deviance at NASA.* Chicago: University of Chicago Press.
9. Hall, J. L., (2003). Columbia and challenger: Organizational failure at NASA. *Space Policy, 19,* 239–247.
10. Birkland, T. A., (2004). Learning and policy improvement after disaster: The case of aviation security. *American Behavior Science, 48,* 341–364.
11. Deep Water Horizon Study Group (2011). Final Report on the Investigation of the Macando Well Blowout (1 Mar 2011).
12. Neshkati, N., (1991). Human factors in large scale technological systems: Three-mile Island, Bhopal, Chernobyl. *Organ Environment, 5,* 133–154.
13. Furuta, K., Sasou, K., Kubota, R., Ujita, H., Shuto, Y., & Yagi, E. (2000). Human factor analysis of JCO criticality accident. *Cognition Technology and Work, 2.*
14. Homsma, G. J., Van Dyck, C., De Gilder, D., Koopman, P. L., & Elfring, T. (2009). Learning from error: The influence of error incident characteristics. *Journal of Business Research, 62,* 115–122.
15. Scheck, B., Neufeld, P., & Dwyer, J. (2000). *Actual innocence: Five days to execution and other dispatches from the wrongly convicted* (Vol. 264). New York: Random House.
16. Garrett, B. (2011). *Convicting the innocent: Where criminal prosecutions go wrong.* Cambridge: Harvard University Press.
17. Ede, R., & Shephard, E. (2000). *Active defense.* London: Law Society Publishing.
18. Leo, R. a. (2008). *Police interrogation and American justice.* Cambridge: Harvard University Press.
19. Kassin, S., Drizin, S., Grisso, T., Gudjonsson, G., Leo, R., & Redlich, A. (2010). police-induced confessions: Risk factors and recommendations. *Law and Human Behavior, 34,* 3–38.
20. Gould, J. B., & Leo, R. A. (2010). One hundred years of getting it wrong: Wrongful convictions after a century of research. *Journal of Criminal Law and Criminology, 100,* 825–868.

21. Steblay, N., Dysert, J., Fulero, S., & Lindsay, R. C. L. (2001). Eyewitness accuracy rates in police show-up and line-up presentations: A meta-analytic comparison. *Law and Human Behavior, 27*, 523–540.
22. Yarmey, D. A., Yarmey, M. J., & Yarmey, L. A. (1996). Accuracy of eyewitness identifications in showups and lineups. *Law and Human Behavior, 20*, 459–477.
23. Connors, E., Lundregan, T., Miller, N., & Mcewan, T. (1996). *Convicted by Juries, exonerated by science: Case studies in the use of DNA evidence to establish innocence after trial.* Washington, D.C.: National Institute of Justice.
24. Kassin, S., M. (2006). A critical appraisal of modern police interrogations. In T. Williamson (Ed.), Investigative interviewing: Rights, research, regulation (pp. 207–228). Devon, UK: Willan Publishing (Chapter 11).
25. Hara, P. O'. (2005). Why law enforcement organizations fail: Mapping the organizational 243 fault lines in policing, at 15 . Carolina: Carolina Academic Press
26. Bryett, K., Harrison, A., & Shaw, J. (1994). *The role and functions of police in Australia (Vol. 2).* Sydney: Butterworths.
27. Friedrich, R. J. (1980). *Police use of force: Individuals, situations and organizations. The Annals of the American Academy of Political and Social Science, 452*, 82–97.
28. Gottfredson, M. R., & Gottfredson, D. M. (1988). *Decision making in criminal justice: Toward the rational exercise of discretion.* New York: Plenum Press.
29. Konecni, V. J., & Ebbesen, E. B. (1984). The mythology of legal decision making. *International Journal of Law Psychiatry, 7*, 5–18.
30. Packer, H. L. (1968). *The limits of the criminal sanction, Chapter 8, two models of criminal process* (Vol. 149). Palo Alto: Stanford University Press.
31. Sagan, S. (1993). *The Limits of Safety.* Princeton: Princeton University Press.
32. Doyle, J. (2012). *Learning about learning from error, 14 ideas in American policing* (6th ed.). Washington, D.C.: Police Foundation.
33. Reason, J. (1997). *Managing the risks of organizational accidents.* Aldershot: Ashgate.
34. Reason, J. (1998). Achieving a safe culture. *Work Stress, 12*, 293–306.
35. Vincent, G. A., & Bark, P. (1995). Accident investigation: Discovering why things go wrong. in G., A. Vincent (Ed.), *Clinical risk management.* London: BMJ Publishing Group.
36. Doyle, J. (2012). Learning about learning from error, Ideas in American Policing. *14*, 1–15. Washington, D.C.: Police Foundation.
37. Holtz, L. E. (2011). *The state law enforcement handbook* (2nd ed., p. 256). U.S.: Lexis/Nexis.
38. U.S. Department of Justice. (1999). *Eyewitness evidence: a guide for law enforcement* (p. 27). U.S.: National Institute of Justice.

# Chapter 2
# Theoretical Framework

## 2.1 Brief Overview

This case is described in terms of James Reason's *organizational accident* framework.[1] An organizational accident is a confluence of human, situational and other contextual circumstances that combine and breach established organizational defenses that have been erected to guard against certain hazards; when breached, those hazards produce harmful outcomes (Fig. 2.1). Failure in an organization generally occurs "…when some operation, employee, policy or process produces results that deviate from expectations in substantial and disruptive ways. Failure encompasses accident, non-performance, corrupt performance and deviant behavior."[2] When an organizational accident occurs, it typically takes on four dimensions—organizational factors, unsafe supervision, preconditions for unsafe acts and unsafe acts—that consist of both active failures and latent conditions, which under context-specific situations align to allow a given hazard to breach each level of established defense.

An active failure arises when an employee performs an act of commission or an act of omission that is outside the scope of accepted policy or practice, and the result is likely to have immediate and harmful consequences. Active failures arise in two forms, from errors that are unintentional and from violations that are intentional breaches of accepted policy or practice. Although individual employees are the source of active failures and it is their initial conduct and subsequent failure to correct conditions that combine to cause harm, an active failure is often preceded by latent conditions that lay dormant and go unnoticed or are ignored, yet which play a facilitating role in initiating and accelerating the active failure.

Latent conditions are features of the system (e.g., deficient policies, inadequate supervision, under staffing, inadequate training and technical proficiency) that are substandard and have been left undetected or unresolved until the active failure reveals them. While active failures are committed by operators (i.e., police officers) at the sharp end of the system, latent conditions result from decision and indecision by senior- and mid-level police managers and front-line supervisors

---

[1] Reason 1997 [1, 2].
[2] Ref. [3]

J. Shane, *Learning from Error in Policing*, SpringerBriefs in Policing, DOI: 10.1007/978-3-319-00041-1_2, © The Author(s) 2013

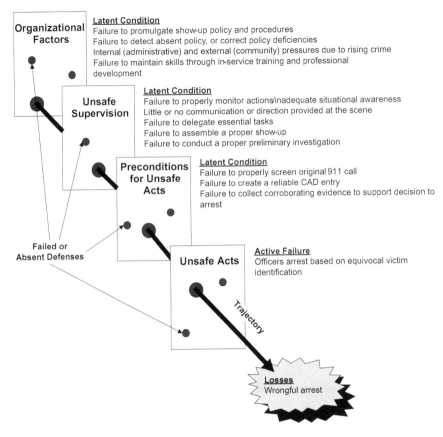

**Fig. 2.1** Example of a wrongful arrest following a police show-up framed by the organizational accidental model (modified from [14])

inside the organization and by regulators outside the organization. Latent conditions often lay undetected partly from failure of imagination and complacency because harmful errors are rare events, but also because reviewing and challenging established policies and processes that seem to be working well may be regarded as pointless by managers and subsequently dismissed.[3]

Active failures are guarded against by purposely designing the organization with deep defenses in mind to ensure unsafe acts are stopped before they

---

[3] Reason 1997 [1], at 6, *The Dangers of the "Unrocked Boat,"* (describing the gradual erosion of safety and the slide into complacency); Ref. [4] (assumption-based planning is intended to counter this complacency); *see also* Reason 1998 [3] (moving toward the ideal informed safety culture includes "not forgetting to be afraid" simply because an accident is a rare event, or has not occurred); Ref. [4, 5]; THE 9/11 COMMISSION REPORT, at 339, 344–348 (citing the "failure of imagination" as a contributing factor of the U.S. Government's failure to act).

materialize, or at least corrected before they cause someone harm. The defenses police departments implement are "soft" in that they are a combination of people and paper: "legislation, regulatory surveillance [scheduled and unscheduled audits, integrity tests and inspections], rules and procedures, training, drills and briefings, administrative controls, licensing, certification and supervisory oversight."[4] When successive gaps or weaknesses align under specific circumstances, the hazard that is sought to be guarded against now comes into damaging contact with people or property and harmful consequences ensue.

## 2.2 Organizational Factors

Organizational factors reside at the top of the hierarchy and are controlled by executives and managers. The organization takes its design from rational planning exercises undertaken by the top management, which are reflected in Luther Gulick's acronym POSDCORB,[5] where administrators and managers set the climate, decide how to structure the organization and allocate resources to achieve the desired mission. How resources are apportioned impacts the principles embedded in the agency's operating policies. For example, systematically underfunding the agency leads to inadequate staffing; inadequate staffing creates personnel shortages; personnel shortages create gaps at the operating level, where shortcuts and other risky practices become normalized to satisfy competing demands caused by internal and external pressure for productivity. When this occurs, safety is likely compromised.

Similarly, creating and maintaining policy is a matter of directing the organization. When policy is deficient, or entirely absent and left undetected, individual police officers and supervisors are not left with sufficient guidelines on how to operate in a given circumstance. Although an insufficient policy or the failure to promulgate a written policy does not absolve the individual officer from personal responsibility, it does serve as a precursor (i.e., latent condition) that facilitates an unsafe act, which ultimately leads to harmful consequences. Policies are the organization's first line of defense to unsafe acts; they are the bedrock upon which democratic policing is built in rule-of-law societies and must comport with the legal and ethical constraints imposed by the substantive law, procedural law and accepted industry standards. Policies act as safeguards to counterbalance the competing constructs of production and safety in an organization. As the police bureaucracy grows more diversified with specialized units, production increases as

---

[4] Reason 1997 [1] at 8 (contrast with "hard" defenses, which are defined as physical devices such as locks, alarms and warning lights).

[5] LUTHER GULICK, NOTES ON THE THEORY OF ORGANIZATION (L. Gulick and L. Urwick Eds., Papers on the Science of Administration 1936 at 3–35, Institute of Public Administration) (POSDCORB: planning, organizing, staffing, directing, coordinating, reporting and budgeting).

does the likelihood for exposure to hazards.[6] Ideally, as production increases, there should be a corresponding increase in safety (i.e., sound operating policies, supervision and span of control[7]), yet they rarely receive parity; production typically wins.

In short, organizational factors inevitably become a "…quality, reliability or safety problem for someone somewhere in the system at some later point."[8]

## 2.3 Unsafe Supervision

Police supervision is organized at graduated (hierarchical) levels to ensure the procedural, legal and ethical mandates embedded in policies are upheld. Supervisors do this by making decisions and monitoring line staff by lending their knowledge and expertise to specific situations. Supervision at each level provides another layer of defense against unsafe acts, and supervisors are entrusted to oversee operations and make corrections—both proactively and reactively—when warranted. By virtue of their status, supervisors have the authority and responsibility to direct the front-line officers' actions to ensure appropriate action is taken, to provide subordinate personnel with advice and technical assistance, as well as review their work to ensure proper procedures are followed and reasonable standards of workmanship are maintained. Although supervisors may delegate assignments to subordinate personnel with the authority to complete the assignment, the supervisor does not delegate responsibility; the supervisor remains accountable for his or her actions and those of the subordinate personnel, which is a public expectation rooted in accountability.[9]

If a police supervisor is not well versed in policies and practices due to inadequate training, personal preparation or inexperience, then they are likely to make decisions based on outdated information, or rely on outmoded practices or standards that leave a gap sufficient for an unsafe act to breach. When this occurs throughout the supervisory chain, the intended organizational defense (i.e., supervision) is compromised and can do little to stop the accident's trajectory. When higher supervisory elements of the organization are aware of an individual supervisor's

---

[6] Production hazards in policing are engaging in arrests, traffic stops, field interviews, custodial interrogations, identification procedures, search and seizure activities particularly search warrant service, vehicular pursuits, using force, employing confidential informants and other similar enforcement actions; *see also* Ref. [4–6] (describing the competing interests of production and safety).

[7] Span of control is defined as the maximum number of subordinate personnel a single supervisor can effectively manage *see* Refs. [7, 8].

[8] Reason, 1997 [1] at 12.

[9] Accountability means to subordinate to a process, where the subject bears an obligation or willingness to accept responsibility and to proffer a statement or explanation of the reasons, causes or motives for their actions; *See* Iannone [7, 8] at 25–28 and Schroeder, Lombardo & Strollo [7, 8] at 26–29, [7, 8].

incompetence and promote the supervisor, or allow the supervisor to continue in their role without remedial training or removing the supervisor from that role, then the organization may assume vicarious liability for negligent supervision and training; in the case of willful disregard of the law or policy, a supervisor may be held liable for malfeasance, misfeasance or civil rights violations.[10]

## 2.4  Preconditions for Unsafe Acts

Preconditions for unsafe acts involve environmental and personnel factors that account for poor tactics, competing interests and inadequate personal prepared-ness, which facilitates a breach in the organization's defenses. In the policing context, the environmental factors include the physical surroundings, political climate and the technical interface. The physical environment can present unan-ticipated hazards that can reduce visual cues or become distracting, which leads to perceptual errors at a time when crucial decisions must be made. The political climate influences the style of policing adopted by the agency, which affects the organizational culture and ultimately how personnel behave.[11] Police chiefs take their cue for organizational structure and institutional behavior from community sentiment that is expressed through elected officials (most often the mayor and council members). Three styles of policing emerged from early research in this area—watchman, legalistic and service.[12] The watchman style is typically found in working-class communities and emphasizes order maintenance, where the pre-ferred method to resolve conditions is discretion, resorting to arrest is the last option. The legalistic style is typically found in communities with high crime and emphasizes formal action and less officer discretion by invoking the law and effecting arrests. The service style is typically found in affluent communities and is oriented toward discretion and addressing community needs. Although each policing style accepts arrests and enforcement actions differently as a measure of policing style, overall crime rate is usually a strong predictor of arrest[13] and there is likely to be some degree of overlap among styles instead of mutual exclusivity.

---

[10] *See* 42 USC §1983—Action for Deprivation of Rights; *see also* Monroe v. Pape, 365 U.S. 167, 81 S. Ct. 473 (1961) and Monell v. Department of Social Services. 436 U.S. 658 (1978) (establishing that local governing bodies and local officials can be sued directly under §1983 for damages, where their edicts or acts may fairly be said to represent *de facto* policy. Monell cases are informally referred to as "pattern or practice" suits even though the custom or pattern at issue has not received formal approval through the government's official decision-making channels); *see also* Williams v. Anderson 599 F. 2d 923 (1979), Ford v. Byrd 544 F.2d 194 (1976) (holding management, the police agency and the jurisdiction responsible for acts committed by subordinate personnel); Ref. [9].

[11] Ref. [10]; for an extended discussion of police culture and cultural deviation see O'Hara [3] at 137–179.

[12] Wilson [10].

[13] Ref. [11]

The personnel factors encompass mental and physiological states and technical job knowledge required to carry out the police function in a given situation. Adverse mental conditions include mental fatigue, overconfidence, complacency and physiological states such as physical fatigue, pharmacological and medical conditions that impair performance. The technical environment rests heavily on knowledge of the substantive and procedural law for direction, which is typically embedded in agency rules, regulations and policies.

As a matter of course, the environmental factors shape the operational tempo; when hazardous conditions are present, the operational tempo increases, which requires swifter decisions that may be based on incomplete information or memory lapses eventually compromising safety. As hazardous conditions subside and the scene becomes "secure," the operational tempo slows giving way to decisions based on more complete information and rational thought.[14] In each instance, the demand for technical knowledge is present but is more pressing in the former than the latter. As the police establish control over a situation and slow the pace of the events, they gain an advantage in their decision making and they are better able to apply their technical knowledge as the event unfolds.

The public demands that police officers demonstrate a minimum level of competence before they are permitted to make decisions on their behalf. Once they are admitted to practice, they must undergo periodic professional development to maintain or strengthen their business acumen so their technical competencies do not evanesce. Periodic training ensures police officers are knowledgeable about changes in the laws, policies and procedures that govern their work product, but most importantly that each officer is forearmed with knowledge that allows them to scrupulously monitor the competing interests of crime control and due process.

## 2.5  Unsafe Acts

Unsafe acts are typically the proximate cause of an organizational accident and include errors and violations, where errors are unintentional and violations are intentional. Errors take many forms, whereas violations are subdivided into two forms, the routine and the exceptional.[15]

Skill-based errors result from divided attention or memory lapses, where the error is inadvertent (e.g., not paying attention to the task). Decision errors represent intentional behavior that proceeds as planned, although the plan itself is poorly designed or inappropriate for the situation. These unsafe acts represent the acts or omissions of individual officers who are "well intentioned," but either lack important technical knowledge or simply make poor choices; in either case, harm results.

---

[14] Refs. [12, 13]
[15] Refs. [14–16]

Decision errors typically take two forms, procedural errors and poor choice errors. Procedural decision errors involve sequencing, where structured tasks contain successive steps that must be executed to ensure safety.[16] These errors arise when operators fail to observe accepted industry standards for a given activity. Poor choice errors occur when the decision-maker is confronted with a situation and has options for proceeding, but selects an option that is influenced by external pressure, time, inexperience or insufficient knowledge. In an effort to expedite the matter, or "go along to get along," the individual chooses a path that ultimately proves harmful.

Perceptual errors occur when interpretation differs from reality. Police officers interpret events within their ken, which is informed by personal and vicarious experience and training. They will often rely on perceptual shorthand to sift through rapidly evolving facts that may be mixed with lies, unusual circumstances or other ambiguities that distort reality. When this occurs, the officer is left to make a decision based on incomplete information, which inevitably increases the risk of committing a harmful error. Importantly, the distorted reality confronting the officer is not the perceptual error; rather, the officer's reaction to the distortion is what triggers or accelerates the error.

Hardware errors relate to the quality and availability of equipment necessary to execute the police function. An operational hardware error may occur when equipment is misused based on training or manufacturer's recommendation; however, a latent hardware error occurs when necessary equipment is aging, or is not available (e.g., loss, theft, damage or has never been purchased). Communications errors occur when pertinent information is not collected and transmitted to support the operation, or when instructions are not conveyed or not received and understood by operators from someone who has relevant knowledge or situational awareness. Goal conflict errors arise from competing interests held at different levels of the organization: (1) at the individual level, operators may be preoccupied with or distracted by personal matters; (2) at the work-group level, informal norms and practices may conflict with formal policies; and (3) at the organizational level, there may be disparity between production and safety. Goal conflict may arise formally through written documents or tacitly through pressure from managers and supervisors.

Design errors occur when there is a failure to provide direction through published policy or procedure (the knowledge gap). Maintenance management errors occur when there is a failure to maintain or upgrade individual skills through relevant and timely training, or to maintain equipment at specified intervals dictated by law, policy or manufacturer's recommendation. Lastly, training errors occur when personnel fail to comprehend the material, or when training is downgraded in quantity or quality leaving a gap between innovation and practice.

While errors are unintentional and occur within the confines of the law and established policy, violations are intentional and occur as a matter of routine and

---

[16] Ref. [17]

exception. Routine violations occur as a matter of accepted past practice and may be tolerated by the organization.[17] Institutionally accepted past practice typical exists when at least three elements are present: (1) clarity and consistency; (2) longevity and repetition; and (3) acceptability. Clarity and consistency define how a given course of conduct is viewed by the organization. When particular conduct is vague or is contradicted as often as it is followed, then it does not qualify as a practice. However, where employees respond in a predictable manner to a given condition, then their conduct will likely develop into a practice. Consistent conduct must be accompanied by a period of time sufficient to establish a pattern of repetitive behavior. Isolated incidents do not establish a practice; however, defining how frequently and over what period of time the conduct must occur before it qualifies as a practice is a value judgment and does not lend itself to a precise formula. Lastly, employees and supervisors alike must know the conduct exists *and* must regard it as a legitimate and customary means of handling a situation. Whether passed along in oral history or deed, conduct becomes acceptable when employees and supervisors acquiesce to it and do not complain about its existence. It is this conduct that partly explains how *Monell* cases (i.e., pattern or practice lawsuits) arise and how *de facto* policy is established. Accepted past practice implicates the supervisory chain insofar as the practice is typically widely known and often condoned by, if not practiced by management, which is tantamount to "bending the rules" and while it "takes two to Tango," management bears the responsibility for stopping it.

Exceptional violations occur, not as a matter of routine, but as a departure from established authority that amounts to an isolated incident, which neither indicates routine practice or management-sanctioned behavior.[18] Exceptional in this context does not refer to the egregiousness of the violation; rather, the violation is exceptional because it is neither characteristic of the individual, nor sanctioned by management. Although uncovering and correcting routine violations should be a matter of practice during periodic audits and inspections, exceptional violations are virtually impossible to predict since they are anomalous and do not reveal themselves through established patterns.

## References

1. Reason, J. (1997). *Managing the risks of organizational accidents*. Aldershot: Ashgate.
2. Reason, J. (1998). Achieving a safe culture. *Work Stress, 12*, 293–306.
3. Hara, P. O'. (2005). *Why law enforcement organizations fail: Mapping the organizational fault lines in policing, at 15*. Durham, NC: Carolina Academic Press.
4. Dewar, A. J. (1993). *Assumption-based planning: A tool for reducing avoidable surprises*. Santa Monica, Ca: Rand.

---

[17]  Reason 1997 [3].

[18]  Reason 1997 [3].

5. Ramanujam, R., & Goodman, P. S. (2003). Latent errors and adverse organizational consequences: A conceptualization. *Journal of Organizational Behaviour, 24*, 815–836.

6. Goh, Y., Love, P., Brown, H., & Spickett, J. (2012). Organizational accidents: A systemic model of production versus protection. *Journal of Organizational Behaviour, 49*, 52–76.

7. Iannone, N. F. (1987). *Supervision of police personnel* (4th ed., pp. 24–25). Upper Saddle River, NJ: Prentice Hall.

8. Schroeder, D. J., Lombardo, F., & Strollo, J. (1995). *Management and supervision of law enforcement* (pp. 34–35). Binghampton, NY: Gould Publications.

9. Kappeler, V. E. (1997). *Critical issues in police civil liability* (2nd ed., pp. 425–435). Long Grove, IL: Waveland.

10. Wilson, J. Q. (1968). *Varieties of police behavior* (pp. 161–171). Cambridge, MA: Harvard University Press.

11. Chappell, T., MacDonald, J. M., Manz, P. W., & Spickett, J. (2006). The organizational determinants of police arrest decisions. *Crime & Delinquency, 52*, 287–306.

12. Isenberg, D. J. (1981). Some effects of time pressure on vertical structure and decision-making accuracy in small groups. *Organizational Behaviour Human Performance, 27*, 119–134.

13. Kelly, J. R., & McGrath, J. E. (1985). Effects of time limits and task types on task performance and interaction of four-person groups. *Journal of Personnel Social Psychology, 49*, 395–407.

14. Reason, J. (1990). *Human error* (pp. 631–640). Cambridge, MA: Cambridge University Press.

15. Rasmussen, J. (1982). Human errors: A taxonomy for describing human malfunction in industrial installations. *Journal of Occupational Accidents, 4*, 311–333.

16. Shappel, S. A., & Wiegman, D. A. (2000). *The human factors analysis and classification system–HFACS* (pp. 1–15). Washington, D.C.: Federal Aviation Administration.

17. Orasanu, J. (1993). Decision-making in the cockpit. In E. L. Wiener, B. G. Kanki, & R. L. Helmrich (Eds.), *Cockpit resource management* (pp. 137–172). U.S.A.: Academic.

# Chapter 3
# Data and Methodology

This research uses a mixed method design[1] to present a deep narrative account of facts that offer context (qualitative), supplemented by statistical data (quantitative) that offer breadth. Mixed methodology was selected for the strength of triangulation to elaborate and clarify the findings and to generate greater understanding about how errors in policing might occur. The source documents for the analysis appear in Table 3.1.

In addition to the written documents, there were 2 h, 33.6 min of audio and video recordings of police interrogations and interview statements taken from witnesses and one offender, and 105 crime scene photographs. These data were analyzed to corroborate statements made by the witnesses and police officers and to compare observed actions to expectations that are embedded in law and policy.

In total, these are the usual and customary data necessary to document and understand the sequence of events, actions, and consequences arising from such an incident. These data help to determine the onset of the event and law enforcement's reaction, particularly to: (1) establish the foundation and basis for police operating practices; (2) determine the extent of the response by the City Police Department and the County Prosecutor's Office; (3) compare observed actions of the officers against the policies upon which those actions are predicated; and (4) determine whether or not the response comported with reasonable and accepted police practices from a national perspective including the contextual factors known to the police at the time certain decisions were made, the contributing factors and the reasonableness of the response.

## 3.1 Qualitative Design

The qualitative portion describes the setting, details of the incident, maps the failure points, and treats the entire case as the unit of analysis ($n = 1$). The single-case study design also known as the critical instance design was used in this research.[2]

---

[1] Maruna [1] and Johnson and Onwuegbuzie [2].
[2] *See generally* U.S. GENERAL ACCOUNTING OFFICE CASE STUDY EVALUATIONS, at 45, (Washington, D.C., November 1990); Yin [3].

J. Shane, *Learning from Error in Policing*, SpringerBriefs in Policing,
DOI: 10.1007/978-3-319-00041-1_3, © The Author(s) 2013

**Table 3.1** Source documents

| Documents | Pages | % |
|---|---|---|
| Deposition transcripts | 2,475 | 76.18 |
| Court reports and transcripts | 450 | 13.85 |
| City police department policies | 72 | 2.22 |
| County prosecutor's office reports and memoranda | 48 | 1.48 |
| Answers to interrogatories and amended complaints | 46 | 1.42 |
| Official City police department reports | 38 | 1.17 |
| Defendants' expert report | 31 | 0.95 |
| Civil complaints | 27 | 0.83 |
| Language transcription reports (from Spanish to English) | 17 | 0.52 |
| State law enforcement policies and memoranda | 14 | 0.43 |
| Training records | 8 | 0.25 |
| Applicable law enforcement standards (local, state, and national) | 8 | 0.25 |
| State public defender's reports | 7 | 0.22 |
| State case law digest | 4 | 0.12 |
| Fingerprint cards | 3 | 0.09 |
| Criminal complaints | 1 | 0.03 |
| *Total* | 3,249 | 100 |

The case study method is an approach for "learning about a complex instance based on a comprehensive understanding of that instance obtained by extensive description and analysis of that instance taken as a whole and in its context" instead of just delivering "variables."[3] This method involves "thick" descriptions from multiple sources that form a qualitative result, meaning it involves descriptions or distinctions based on qualities or attributes rather than numerical data or quantities, as well as deeper insight into police practices.[4] The single-case method is appropriate when the instance under examination is of unique or critical interest; (1) this case involves a first-degree armed robbery, where the victim was assaulted across the head with a piece of wood; (2) one alleged offender was misidentified and subsequently jailed for 4 months; (3) the alleged offenders were indicted for armed robbery and the prosecution had begun; (4) the indictment was dismissed against all three alleged offenders, not just the offender who was misidentified, following an in-court identification hearing[5]; and (5) the case was never prosecuted.

To identify the variables associated with the active failure (i.e., wrongful arrest), the data were analyzed by means of process tracing, which is a method that

---

[3] *See* U.S. GAO [4], at 15; *see also* Blumer [5].

[4] Baxter and Jack [6], Eisenhardt [7], Flyvbjerg [8] and Baker [9].

[5] As part of U.S. jurisprudence, a hearing is held to determine whether the out-of-court identification was so suggestive that the person making the identification (i.e., victim or witness) may have been mistaken; *see* United States v. Wade, 388 U.S. 218 (1967) (a pretrial hearing in a criminal case to determine whether a witness's identification of the accused (as in a show-up procedure) is tainted due to impermissibly suggestive procedures and is therefore inadmissible as evidence).

examines the intervening process—the causal chain—between the independent variables and the dependent variables.[6] By examining human interaction processes and searching for the links in the causal chain to explain why certain outcomes may have occurred, it is possible to isolate key failure points. Figure 2.1 depicts the empirical focus, where the loss represents the outcome (the dependent variable is the wrongful arrest) and is the starting point for the analysis. The last stage before the loss occurs—unsafe acts—represents the proximate cause of the accident. By tracing the processes in reverse order, it is possible to identify and analyze the independent variables and the influence they have on the outcome variable.

The case was first explored by analyzing the content of the source documents and matching the observed actions and omissions of the officers to the accepted industry standards. The  industry standards were drawn from: (1) applicable case law from the U.S. Supreme Court, U.S. District Courts, U.S. Appellate Courts and state courts that govern policing; (2) model policies from the Commission on Accreditation for Law Enforcement Agencies[7] that establish a set of national professional standards; (3) the City police department's policies that specify procedures for the officers involved; (4) the state's law enforcement policies that govern the officers' actions and omissions; and (5) the accepted principles of criminal investigation, police management, and supervision. To be deemed a failure point, the observed action or omission must have violated a law, policy, or accepted practice during the preliminary or follow-up investigation. The failure points were situated according to the four aspects of organizational accident theory described in Fig. 2.1 and also categorized according to the general failure types (GFT) shown in Table 3.2. To strengthen validity, the identified failure points were crosschecked against the literature for accepted industry standards on criminal investigations, police management and supervision verify the appropriate category of failure; several authoritative sources were used to establish convergent validity for the construct under examination.[8]

## 3.2 Quantitative Design

To supplement the qualitative findings, quantitative indicators of agency role, error type, and investigative stage were identified and coded ($n = 49$). The observed failure points were matched to the failure categories according to James Reason's

---

[6] George and Bennett [10].

[7] (CALEA is a U.S.-based voluntary credentialing authority that exists to improve the delivery of public safety services, primarily by: maintaining a body of standards, developed by public safety practitioners, covering a wide range of up-to-date public safety initiatives; establishing and administering an accreditation process; and recognizing professional excellence. *See* www.calea.org/content/commission retrieved on March 15, 2012).

[8] *See specifically* Adams [11], Hale [12], International Association of Chiefs of Police [13], Giacalone [14], Lyman [15], Sonne [16], National Institute of Justice [17], Swanson et al. [18], Geberth [19] and Hess and Orthmann [20].

**Table 3.2** Classification of observed failures during the preliminary and follow-up investigation according to the general failure type categories ($n = 49$)

| Failure category | Conceptual definition | Observed failure | Investigative stage | Agency role | Error type |
|---|---|---|---|---|---|
| Procedural error ($n = 35$) | Issues related to the quality, accuracy, relevance, availability and workability of procedures | Failed to establish sufficient connection between the alleged offenders and the tertiary crime scene (the vehicle) | Preliminary | Management supervision | Omission |
| | | Failed to examine the victim about his medical condition after the assault | Preliminary | Management supervision | Omission |
| | | Failed to maintain the inner perimeter at the secondary crime scene | Preliminary | Management supervision | Omission |
| | | Failed to properly document each crime scene through a crime scene log | Preliminary | Management supervision | Omission |
| | | Failed to search inside the apartment complex, where a female reported seeing three males matching the offenders' description run | Preliminary | Management supervision | Omission |
| | | Failed to preserve each crime scene | Preliminary | Management supervision | Omission |
| | | Failed to document sworn statements from some witnesses and others in a timely manner | Preliminary | Management supervision | Omission |
| | | Failed to conduct a neighborhood canvass | Preliminary | Management supervision | Omission |
| | | Failed to adequately process each crime scene | Preliminary | Management supervision | Omission |
| | | Failed to adequately search each crime scene | Preliminary | Management supervision | Omission |
| | | Failed to collect corroborating evidence to support the prosecution | Preliminary | Management supervision | Omission |
| | | Conducted an unlawful search of the tertiary crime scene (the vehicle), per state law | Follow-up | Line | Act |

(continued)

**Table 3.2** (continued)

| Failure category | Conceptual definition | Observed failure | Investigative stage | Agency role | Error type |
|---|---|---|---|---|---|
| | | Unlawfully destroyed all investigative notes taken by detectives, per state law | Follow-up | Line | Act |
| | | Failed to collect any physical or testimonial evidence to connect the offenders to the robbery (primary crime scene), the vehicle (tertiary crime scene), and the apartment (secondary crime scene) | Follow-up | Line | Omission |
| | | Failed to conduct further surveillance to develop evidence or information | Follow-up | Line | Omission |
| | | Created inaccurate CAD record entries | Preliminary | Line | Act |
| | | Failed to document a sworn statement from the auditory witness discovered inside the retail store during the robbery | Follow-up | Line | Omission |
| | | Failed to document search and seizure activities by the lead detective | Follow-up | Line | Omission |
| | | Failed to document a sworn statement from the alibi witness for the plaintiff | Follow-up | Line | Omission |
| | | Failed to employ confidential informants to help develop evidence or information | Follow-up | Line | Omission |
| | | Failed to locate and identify the anonymous witness who pointed out the vehicle (tertiary crime scene) and said three males emerged from that vehicle | Follow-up | Line | Omission |
| | | Failed to initiate a second interrogation of the plaintiff, his accomplices and to re-interview witnesses to support the prosecution when the original interrogation failed | Follow-up | Line | Omission |

(continued)

**Table 3.2** (continued)

| Failure category | Conceptual definition | Observed failure | Investigative stage | Agency role | Error type |
|---|---|---|---|---|---|
| | | Failed to locate and interview the witness who saw three males run inside the multi-family house | Follow-up | Line | Omission |
| | | Failed to interview the accomplice's alibi witness for information and knowledge about the case she may have had | Follow-up | Line | Omission |
| | | Failed to interview the victim for his version of the events | Follow-up | Line | Omission |
| | | Failed to investigate the alibi proffered by the accomplice's alibi witness that undermined the prosecution | Follow-up | Line | Omission |
| | | Failed to investigate the alibi proffered by the plaintiff's alibi witness that undermined the prosecution | Follow-up | Line | Omission |
| | | Failed to locate and interview the female friend of the accomplice's alibi witness who was found at the multi-family house for her involvement or information | Follow-up | Line | Omission |
| | | Failed to locate and interview the male roommate of the accomplice's alibi witness for his involvement or information | Follow-up | Line | Omission |
| | | Failed to obtain search warrants or written consent to search for evidence to support the prosecution | Follow-up | Line | Omission |
| | | Failed to preserve original 911 call to support the investigation | Preliminary | Line | Omission |
| | | Failed to preserve original police radio transmissions to support the investigation | Preliminary | Line | Omission |
| | | Failed to properly log into evidence video statements of the alleged accomplices | Follow-up | Line | Omission |

(continued)

**Table 3.2** (continued)

| Failure category | Conceptual definition | Observed failure | Investigative stage | Agency role | Error type |
|---|---|---|---|---|---|
| Decision error—poor choice ($n = 3$) | Intentional behavior that proceeds as planned, although the plan itself is poorly designed or inappropriate for the situation. Poor choice errors occur when the decision maker is confronted with a situation and has options for proceeding, but selects an option that is influenced by external pressure, time, inexperience, or insufficient knowledge | Failed to re-canvass the primary and secondary crimes scenes and escape routes for additional witnesses or evidence | Follow-up | Line | Omission |
| | | Failed to visit the primary crime scene as part of the investigation | Follow-up | Line | Omission |
| | | Accepted and endorsed deficient and incomplete investigative reports submitted by the lead detective | Follow-up | Management supervision | Act |
| | | Effected an arrest based on equivocal victim identification without any corroborating evidence | Preliminary | Management supervision | Act |
| | | Failed to summon sufficient personnel from the detective division to support the preliminary investigation | Preliminary | Management supervision | Omission |
| Decision error—procedural ($n = 1$) | Intentional behavior that proceeds as planned, although the plan itself is poorly designed or inappropriate for the situation. Procedural decision errors involve sequencing, where structured tasks contain successive steps that must be executed to ensure safety | Assembled an improper show-up, contrary to U.S. supreme court decisions | Preliminary | Management supervision | Act |
| Incompatible goal error ($n = 2$) | Three types include (1) individual goal conflicts caused by preoccupation or domestic concerns; (2) group goal conflicts, when the informal norms of a work group are incompatible with the safety goals of the organization; and (3) conflicts at the organizational level in which there is incompatibility between safety and productivity goals | Operating under external pressure for results (i.e., arrests) | Preliminary | Management supervision | Act |
| | | Operating under internal pressure from workload (i.e., volume) | Preliminary | Management supervision | Act |

(continued)

**Table 3.2** (continued)

| Failure category | Conceptual definition | Observed failure | Investigative stage | Agency role | Error type |
|---|---|---|---|---|---|
| Communication error (n = 2) | Three types include (1) system failure in which the necessary channels of communication do not exist, or are not functioning, or are not regularly used; (2) message failures in which the channels exist but the necessary information is not transmitted; (3) reception failures in which the channels exist, but the right message is sent, but it is either misinterpreted by the recipient or arrives to late | Failed to communicate and issue specific instructions to officers at the scene | Preliminary | Management supervision | Omission |
| | | Failed to delegate tasks to available officers (i.e., coordination and direction) | Preliminary | Management supervision | Omission |
| Defense error (n = 2) | Failures in detection, warning, personnel protection, recovery, containment, escape, and rescue | Failed to detect investigative deficiencies in report writing and tasks | Follow-up | Management supervision | Omission |
| | | Failed to detect the need for a policy on show-ups | Preliminary | Management supervision | Omission |
| Design error (n = 2) | A failure that leads directly to an error or violation. Three types include (1) a failure on part of the designer to provide external guidance (the knowledge gulf); (2) designed objects are often opaque with regard to their inner workings (the execution gulf); and (3) the failure designed items to provide feedback to the user (the evaluation gulf) | Failed to promulgate a policy on criminal investigation procedures (i.e., knowledge gulf) | Preliminary | Management supervision | Omission |
| | | Failed to promulgate a policy on show-up procedures (i.e., knowledge gulf) | Preliminary | Management supervision | Omission |

(continued)

**Table 3.2** (continued)

| Failure category | Conceptual definition | Observed failure | Investigative stage | Agency role | Error type |
|---|---|---|---|---|---|
| Training error (n = 2) | Seven types including (1) failure to understand training requirements; (2) downgrading training relative to operations; (3) obstructing training; (4) insufficient assessment of results; (5) poor mix of experienced and inexperienced personnel; (6) poor task analysis; and (7) inadequate definition of competence requirements | Lacking basic knowledge of standards and guidelines for conducting criminal investigations | Follow-up | Line | Omission |
| | | Failure to conduct periodic training on show-up procedures | Preliminary | Management supervision | Omission |

GFT, which reflect the workplace and organizational factors that are likely to contribute to an unsafe act (Table 3.2). Not all categories of failures defined by Reason's model were observed, for example, there is no evidence this case experienced any errors in hardware, maintenance management, error-enforcing conditions, housekeeping, or organization.

The data were operationalized according to the following protocol: (1) determine the agency role responsible for the error, either management/supervision or line function, where rational planning, strategy and policy development rest with executive-level officers (management), directing and coordinating activities rest with mid-level and first-line supervisors (supervision) and executing activities rests with front-line officers (line-level); (2) determine the type of error committed, either an act or omission, where an act is overt positive action and an omission is overt negative action; (3) determine the investigative stage when the error occurred, either preliminary or follow-up, where the preliminary investigation begins with the initial receipt of a complaint and extends to the immediate on-scene activities and the follow-up investigation begins when the initial response has ended and detectives assume primary investigative responsibility.

The preliminary investigation is intimately connected to the responsibilities of line-level officers and first-line supervisors, particularly to verify whether a crime has been committed, to identify a perpetrator and preserve the crime scene in the event of prosecution. The preliminary investigative stage also includes any acts or omissions committed at the executive level that precede the initial response since decisions at that level have implications for how officers respond and how they are coordinated and directed once an incident unfolds (Table 3.2). Once coded, the data are summarized then tested for relationships and the prevalence of risk.

## 3.3 Participant Protection

The research site, names of individuals, exact dates, agency names, and locations have been de-identified to preserve confidentiality. Although most of the data are publicly available through various sources, in the interest of ethical responsibility de-identification is best. Given that the study is de-identified it is even more important to ensure accuracy since the sources cannot be readily verified. Wherever possible, verbatim language is provided to convey intent, context, and accuracy; however, where necessary, non-attribution of comments to specific persons or policies was used and policy titles and identifying numbers were removed or referred to in generic terms.[9] Since human subjects are not involved, informed consent was not required.

---

[9]  Seiber [21].

## 3.4 Research Questions

The primary research questions are the following: (1) What are the failure points in the police investigation that facilitated the wrongful arrest? (2) Are acts of commission or acts of omission more prevalent throughout the investigation? (3) Which categories of failure present the greatest risk?

## References

1. Maruna, S. (2010). Mixed method research in criminology: Why not go both ways? In A. Piquero & D. Weisburd (Eds.), *Handbook of quantitative criminology* (pp. 123–140). New York: Springer. Chap. 7.
2. Johnson, R. B., & Onwuegbuzie, A. J. (2004). Mixed methods research: A research paradigm whose time has come. *Education Research, 33*, 14–26.
3. Yin, R. K. (2009). *Case study research: Design and methods* (4th ed., p. 47). CA: Sage.
4. U.S. General Accounting Office. (November 1990). Case study evaluations. Washington, D.C, p. 15
5. Blumer, H. (1956). Sociological analysis and the "Variable". *American Sociological Review, 21*, 683–690.
6. Baxter, P., & Jack, S. (1994). Qualitative case study methodology: Study design and implementation for novice researchers. *The Qualitative Report, 13*, 544–559.
7. Eisenhardt, K. M. (1989). Building theories from case study research. *Academy of Management Review, 14*, 352–550.
8. Flyvbjerg, B. (2006). Five misunderstandings about case-study research. *Qualitative Inquiry, 12*, 219–245.
9. Baker, T. L. (1999). *Doing social research* (3rd ed.). Boston: McGraw-Hill.
10. George, A. L., & Bennett, A. (2005). *Case studies and theory development in the social sciences* (p. 206). Cambridge: MIT Press.
11. Adams, T. F. (2007). *Police field operations* (7th ed.). NJ: Prentice Hall.
12. Hale, C. (1981). *Police patrol: Operations and management.* NJ: Wiley.
13. International Association of Chiefs of Police (1977) The Patrol Operation. 3rd edn. (IACP).
14. Giacalone, J. (2011). *The criminal investigative function: A guide for new investigators.* NY: Looseleaf Law Publications.
15. Lyman, M. D. (2008). Criminal investigation: The art and the science. Upper Saddle River, NJ: Prentice Hall.
16. Sonne, W. J. (2006). *Criminal investigation for the professional investigator.* Boca Raton: CRC Press.
17. National Institute of Justice (2000). Crime scene investigation. National Institute of Justice, NCJ# 178280.
18. Swanson, C., Chemelin, N., & Territo, L. (1996). *Criminal investigation* (6th ed.). NY: McGraw-Hill.
19. Geberth, V. J. (1996). *Practical homicide investigation: Tactics, procedures and forensic techniques.* Boca Raton: CRC Press.
20. Hess, K. M, Orthmann, C. H. (2010). Criminal investigation (9th ed.). Clifton Park, NY: Delmar Cengage.
21. Seiber, J. E. (1992). *Planning ethically responsible research: A guide for students and internal review boards.* CA: Sage.

# Chapter 4
# Details of the Incident

The incident occurred in July 2007, at approximately 3:00 p.m. in a mid-sized U.S. city. A police officer was on patrol in a marked police car in the City when he was approached by an Hispanic male who informed him that he had just been robbed inside his store. The officer broadcasted over the police radio that three White or Hispanic males were seen running east bound on City streets from the store. The offenders were described as:

(1) Male #1. White or Hispanic, white t-shirt and blue jean shorts;
(2) Male #2. White or Hispanic, no shirt, dark jean shorts;
(3) Male #3. White or Hispanic, white t-shirt and blue jeans.

No further description was provided. At or around the time the patrol officer happened upon the victim, the City Police Department also received a 911 telephone call from two unidentified female callers who also alerted them about the robbery.[1] The caller reported that a robbery occurred at the [victim's] store. No further details or description of the offenders were provided.

A second City police officer responded and along the way stopped to speak to a female resident on a nearby residential street who said she observed three males matching the description run from a yard toward an apartment building located on another neighborhood street. The first responding officer then broadcasted over the radio that he was told by an anonymous citizen that the offenders were seen running past a parked vehicle on a nearby street. The officer obtained the ownership information about the vehicle, which was a female resident of a nearby neighborhood. The first two officers responded and were joined by a third officer; all three met at the woman's home, a three family house with a basement, first floor and second floor apartment. The vehicle's owner said she parked her car near a school in City. She was asked if anyone was inside the house with her and she replied "no." She then provided verbal consent for officers to look inside her

---

[1] The account of the robbery was taken directly from official police reports showing what the police knew and when they knew it. Because the details in the official reports about the officers' actions are sparse, information gaps were closed from data embedded in other source documents. Where appropriate, specific identifiers have been removed or renamed generically. The original 911 telephone call was transcribed and appears in a report prepared by the state's public defender's office.

house. One police officer entered the house and found an Hispanic male matching the original description in one room.

Around the same time, a second officer heard a noise coming from the basement area. He proceeded to the basement and spoke to the occupant, an Hispanic male, who was inside a separate apartment. When the occupant opened the door, the officer noticed an Hispanic male seated on a couch wearing a white t-shirt and blue jeans. The officer asked the occupant of the apartment how long the other man had been there and he replied "15 minutes." The officer advised the occupant that "...there was a robbery and that a vehicle which was involved came out of this address." The officer also "...advised him that the individual in his apartment matched the descriptions of one of the suspects." The officer advised the Hispanic male matching the description of one of the offenders what was happening and asked him to "...step outside." The officer escorted the suspect to the front of the house, where he was turned over to a fourth female police officer who had now arrived. The officer then returned to the first floor apartment to continue searching. The officer entered a bathroom and heard the shower water running. The officer asked the female apartment owner who was in the shower and she did not answer. Inside the shower was an Hispanic male who was wearing his underwear and outside the shower on the floor laid his clothes that matched the offender's description, dark jean shorts and white t-shirt. The officer brought this suspect outside, where he joined the other two suspects.

The original responding officer then participated in a show-up identification procedure that was directed by the lieutenant who was now on scene. The victim was driven past the three alleged offenders in a marked police vehicle outside the residence where they were located. The officer advised the victim that the individuals "...may or may not be the individuals involved and to take as much time as he need to make a decision." The officer said in his report that he did not influence the victim's decision. The officer drove past the three alleged offenders as they stood side-by-side and the victim said in Spanish "esos tres son," which means those are the three. The officer then notified the lieutenant via radio that the victim positively identified the three suspects as those who assaulted and robbed him.

All three alleged offenders were arrested and transported to the City police headquarters for processing. A hat belonging to one of the suspects and a wave cap belonging to another suspect were placed into evidence. The victim reportedly lost $50.00 and a cell phone during the robbery. None of the proceeds were recovered.

# Chapter 5
# Show-Up Procedures, Relevant Policy Standards, and Training Standards

## 5.1 Show-Up Procedures

Eyewitness identification has high probative value for the prosecution's case.[1] One method for obtaining eyewitness identification is the show-up procedure. If the prosecution intends to rely on the show-up identification, then the show-up must not be impermissibly suggestive or prone to error, which can lead to misidentification.[2] The United States Supreme Court resolved some questions about the suggestive nature of eyewitness identifications in *United States v. Wade* (1967),[3] which implicates fairness and due process, specifically: (1) the manner in which confrontations for identification are typically conducted; (2) the dangers inherent in eyewitness identification and suggestiveness inherent in the context of the confrontation; and (3) because the likelihood that the accused will often be precluded from reconstructing what occurred, a full hearing on the identification issue at trial is warranted.[4]

The *Wade* decision implies that in-court identifications by a witness of the accused when the accused was previously presented to the witness before trial may be excluded unless the prosecution can establish that any errors that may have occurred during the out-of-court identification were harmless and did not violate the accused's due process rights. If the prosecution fails their argument, then the evidence will likely be suppressed.[5] Although the *Wade* decision benchmarks the suppression standard as it relates to the Fourteenth Amendment, it does not provide police officers with direction on how to conduct the initial out-of-court identification that is in question.

The United States Supreme Court addressed that procedural issue in 1972 in *Neil v. Biggers.*[6] In *Biggers,* the Court addressed the suggestive nature of police show-up identifications and identified a five-prong test to determine whether a

---

[1] Watkins v. Sowders, 449 U.S. 341 (1981).
[2] Steblay, Dysert, Fulero, & Lindsay [1]; Yarmey et al. [2].
[3] United States v. Wade, 388 U.S. 218 (1967).
[4] United States v. Wade at 388 U.S. 229–235 (1967).
[5] United States v. Wade at 388 U.S. 239–243 (1967).
[6] Neil v. Biggers 409 U.S. 188 (1972).

J. Shane, *Learning from Error in Policing*, SpringerBriefs in Policing,
DOI: 10.1007/978-3-319-00041-1_5, © The Author(s) 2013

show-up was so impermissibly suggestive as to suppress its result: (1) the opportunity of the witness to view the criminal at the time of the crime; (2) the witnesses degree of attention; (3) the accuracy of witness's prior description of the criminal; (4) the level of certainty demonstrated by the witness at the confrontation; and (5) the length of time between the crime and the confrontation. Implicit in the decision is the understanding that a show-up procedure should not be undertaken unless the witness has the ability to make a sound identification of the alleged offender. If the witness is uncertain, or cannot cite any identifying characteristics of the alleged offender, which leads to a vague and equivocal identification, then the show-up is likely to be impermissibly suggestive and may be suppressed during pretrial motions; it is incumbent upon the prosecution to demonstrate that the out-of-court identification meets the *Biggers* criteria otherwise they risk suppression.

## 5.2 Relevant Policy Standards

Individual police agencies typically codify criminal procedure in policies then promulgate those policies to ensure all personnel are operating within accepted industry standards. A written policy provides officers with guidance and direction on the legal and ethical limits governing the function, which is intended to increase accountability and consistency in action while concurrently reducing employee autonomy and discretion.[7]

Policy guides decision making by recognizing that as risk increases, discretion decreases. To ensure accountability, important decisions must be either non-discretionary, or must be limited, meaning the policy must limit police officers' and supervisors' discretion. In this regard, policy is an expression of the will of the public. Without a policy, the agency cuts itself off from the public, where there is a tendency to function with unfettered discretion and outside legal and ethical bounds until individual, or collective actions are exposed through scandal, judicial intervention, civil litigation, or government investigation that necessitates reform. A comprehensive policy is an expression of how the agency intends to conduct its affairs and act in specific situations to minimize liability and errors at the agency, supervisory, and line level, particularly when legal and ethical issues arise. Without guidance from the policy, officers do not have uniform procedures to follow, which invites deviance, inconsistency, and misconduct. When police misconduct does occur, it often originates with a failure to promulgate a clear written policy; misconduct is also likely to occur from failing to observe a published policy.

The show-up standard was promulgated in 1972; however, the state, the City police department and the County prosecutor's office had not adopted the standard

---

[7] O' Loughlin [3]; Welsh & Harris [4]; Walker [5] (discussing the potential benefits of confining discretion to promote accountability).

via policy at the time of the incident (2007). The state Attorney General's Office had promulgated a policy governing photographic and live line-up procedures prior to the incident[8]; although the logic of the state's policy extends to show-up procedures (i.e., to avoid being impermissibly suggestive), the policy itself is silent on show-up identifications and the five tenets of *Neil v. Biggers*. The CALEA national standard for show-up identification also did not exist at the time of the incident.[9]

In addition to codifying criminal procedure, industry operating standards are also required to ensure police behavior comports with customary practices. National standards for criminal investigations, evidence collection and crime scene preservation existed prior to the incident through CALEA; however, the City police department had not promulgated a policy for conducting criminal investigations until June 2008. Although a policy on criminal investigations did not exist, the police officers are not absolved from their responsibility to follow longstanding, accepted, and customary police practices; the local standards that were eventually adopted in 2008 following this incident merely codified the accepted industry practice specifically for City police officers.[10]

## 5.3 Training Standards

Training standards exist to ensure police officers acquire and maintain the skills necessary to safely perform the required job functions and to minimize performance errors. Police officers have a duty to act with care; insofar as possible they must avoid injuring citizens in the performance of their duty and they must act reasonably when discharging their duty, which means acting within established law, policy, and accepted practice guidelines. A police officer may be criminally and civilly liable if they act outside established policy and a clear nexus can be established between their performance and a failure on behalf of the agency to follow accepted management, supervision, and/or training standards.

All of the police officers were certified to practice in the state; they each had received basic academy training and some testified at deposition[11] that they

---

[8] The state's policy was promulgated in 2001 and is binding on all police departments. The City police department promulgated a policy on photographic and live line-up procedures in 2008. The policy governs photo and live line-up procedures, but does not cover show-up procedures. The County prosecutor's office promulgated a similar policy that binds all police departments in the County, but is silent on show-up procedures.

[9] *See* CALEA standard 42.2.12, *Show-ups*. The standard was not promulgated until March 26, 2010.

[10] See sources Adams [6], Hale [7], International Association of Chiefs of Police [8], Giacalone [9], Lyman [10], Sonne [11], National Institute of Justice [12], Swanson et al.-[13], Geberth [14] and Hess and Orthmann [15].

[11] The lieutenant, the ranking supervisor in-charge of the preliminary investigation, testified that he received training in advanced criminal investigations at the County Police Academy and he received training in criminal cases and crime scene investigations at the FBI Academy in

received advanced training in: (1) conducting preliminary investigations; (2) collecting evidence; (3) preparing crime scene notes; (4) documenting the crime scene; (5) agency-specific rules, regulations, policies, and procedures; (6) conducting show-up identifications; and (7) searching for physical evidence associated with a crime.[12] Once basic academy training is completed, there is no state mandate that police officers receive periodic training on revisions to standards relating to show-up procedures, changes in procedural law regarding show-ups and new research on the reliability of show-up procedures or criminal investigation techniques; such training is at the police agency's discretion[13] and there is no evidence the officers received any periodic or updated training in show-up procedures or criminal investigations.

# References

1. Steblay, N., Dysert, J., Fulero, S., & Lindsay, R. C. L. (2001). Eyewitness accuracy rates in police show-up and line-up presentations: A meta-analytic comparison. *Law and Human Behavior, 27*, 523–540.
2. Yarmey, D. A., Yarmey, M. J., & Yarmey, L. A. (1996). Accuracy of eyewitness identifications in showups and lineups. *Law and Human Behavior, 20*, 459–477.
3. O'Loughlin, M. G. (1990). What Is Bureaucratic Accountability and How Can We Measure It? *Administration & Society, 22*(3), 275–302.
4. Welsh, W. N., & Harris, P. W. (2004). *Criminal justice policy and planning* (2nd ed., pp. 131–136). Cincinnati, OH: Anderson.
5. Walker, S. (2010). *The New World of Police Accountability.* (pp. 46–49). Thousand Oaks, CA: Sage
6. Adams, T. F. (2007). *Police field operations* (7th ed.). NJ: Prentice Hall.
7. Hale, C. (1981). *Police patrol: Operations and management.* NJ: Wiley.
8. International Association of Chiefs of Police (1977) The Patrol Operation. 3rd edn. (IACP).
9. Giacalone, J. (2011). *The criminal investigative function: A guide for new investigators.* NY: Looseleaf Law Publications.

---

(Footnote 11 continued)

Quantico, Virginia. The lead investigator in this case testified that he "believe[d]" he received one or two training courses in how to conduct investigations as well as how to conduct interviews and interrogation. A supporting detective testified that she was "not certain" about her training history; first, she testified that she did receive training then she testified that she could not recall. Although she may have received training, she testified she is not familiar with the City police department's policy related to identification procedures. The original responding officer testified that he received formal training in show-up identifications in the police academy and during annual in-service training. The second responding officer testified that he received formal training in show-up identifications in the police academy but does not recall any in-service training on the topic.

[12] These training topics are covered in the training course for basic police officer certification promulgated by the state.

[13] In 2000, the state issued a memorandum specifying the categories of mandatory training for police officers; show-up identification is not included and deemed is discretionary, thus not required by the state.

10. Lyman, M. D. (2008). Criminal investigation: The art and the science. Upper Saddle River, NJ: Prentice Hall.
11. Sonne, W. J. (2006). *Criminal investigation for the professional investigator*. Boca Raton: CRC Press.
12. National Institute of Justice (2000). Crime scene investigation. National Institute of Justice, NCJ# 178280.
13. Swanson, C., Chemelin, N., & Territo, L. (1996). *Criminal investigation* (6th ed.). NY: McGraw-Hill.
14. Geberth, V. J. (1996). *Practical homicide investigation: Tactics, procedures and forensic techniques*. Boca Raton: CRC Press.
15. Hess, K. M, Orthmann, C. H. (2010). Criminal investigation (9th ed.). Clifton Park, NY: Delmar Cengage.

# Chapter 6
# Analysis and Findings

The first part of the analysis compares the observed actions of the officers during the investigation to the standards defined by criminal procedure, criminal investigations, police management, and supervision against the organizational accident framework and helps answer the first research question: *what are the failure points in the investigation that facilitated the wrongful arrest?* The second part maps the failure points during the preliminary and follow-up investigations, then tests for relationships and the prevalence of risk, which helps answer the last two research questions: *are acts of commission or acts of omission more prevalent throughout the investigation?* and *which categories of failure present the greatest risk?*

## 6.1 Organizational Factors

### 6.1.1 Policy on Show-Up Procedures was Absent

A policy governing show-ups had not been promulgated by the City police department prior to this incident, a design error that went undetected and created a knowledge gap as the preliminary investigation unfolded. The state Attorney General's policy does not address show-up procedures; the logic of the policy only indirectly implicates show-up procedures. Therefore, the officers did not have a reference document to consult as they faced this legal procedure in the field. To test whether or not the show-up they conducted was impermissibly suggestive and, therefore, could not be relied upon to establish probable cause to arrest, it is necessary to compare the observed actions of the officers to the standard enunciated in *Neil v. Biggers.*

*The opportunity of the witness to the view the criminal at the time of the crime.* The confrontation between the victim and the three alleged offenders took place inside the victim's store at approximately 3 p.m. There are no official records of what the police knew about the victim's opportunity to view the alleged offenders

J. Shane, *Learning from Error in Policing*, SpringerBriefs in Policing, 37
DOI: 10.1007/978-3-319-00041-1_6, © The Author(s) 2013

at the time of the crime, such as (1) the distance between the alleged offenders and the victim[1]; (2) whether the victim was facing the alleged offenders; (3) the order in which the alleged offenders approached the victim and where each alleged offender stood during the robbery; (4) what happened after the victim was assaulted; (5) the length of time the alleged offenders were in front of the victim; (6) the adequacy of the lighting; and (7) whether anything was blocking the victim's view such as merchandise display racks.

One of the alleged offenders reportedly stood at the store's entrance, had his face covered, never approached the victim, and never spoke, but there is no record of the distance between the victim and the alleged offender. In addition, the victim testified that one alleged offender told him to get down on the floor and he complied "...looking down at the floor,"[2] which placed him in a submissive position, so he was no longer looking at the offenders.

One of the supporting detectives from the City police department testified at deposition that she was present along with the original responding police officer during the show-up and she said that the victim told the officers that he only saw the faces of two alleged offenders whom he identified as the two Hispanic males that were located inside the second-floor apartment of the multi-family house. The detective also testified that the victim said he did not see the face of the third offender because the third offender's face was covered and he never positively identified the third offender. The *Wade* hearing transcripts are replete with testimony from the victim that he was either not certain about one alleged offender's identity, could not remember, or did not see the person.

*The witness' degree of attention.* There are no official records documenting how much attention the victim paid to the alleged offenders during their encounter or how much time the alleged offenders spent inside the store during the robbery. The original responding officer testified that the victim did not tell him anything about the weapon that was used nor did he ask about the weapon even though the victim was allegedly assaulted by one of the offenders. Although the officer testified that the victim never said anything about the weapon on the day of the robbery, the victim turned the weapon—a wooden board—over to an investigator from the County prosecutor's office during their investigation in September 2008, more than 1 year later. Empirical research suggests that the presence of a weapon during the commission of a crime tends to reduce the reliability of the victim's identification of the offender because of the victim's focus on it (i.e., "weapon focus") instead of the offender.[3] In this case, the weapon was actually used against the victim to strike him in the head and was not merely displayed, gestured, or threatened.[4]

---

[1]  The crime scene technician from the City police department did not sketch the scene and did not measure distances, which would be expected in such a case.

[2]  This was reported during the *Wade* hearing and attested to by the victim in a sworn declaration.

[3]  *See* Ref. [1].

[4]  (In his deposition, the second responding officer conceded that during a simulated eyewitness identification training exercise while he attended the police academy, some police recruits could not make a positive identification of an offender when a gun was present. The victim testified

Given the very general and limited description of the alleged offenders, no description of the weapon and the fact that the victim was outnumbered and actively being assaulted across the head with a piece of wood support a reasonable inference that his attention was divided and his focus was on his own physical safety, not exclusively the alleged offenders' identity or peripheral details.

*The accuracy of the witness' prior description of the criminal.* The victim never provided any police officers, particularly the first responding officer with any unique physical descriptors—scars, marks, tattoos, body piercings, deformities, or distinctive or unusual physical attributes (e.g., excessively tall, short, heavy, or thin; a limp, a speech impediment, or voice inflection) of the alleged offenders. The victim also never provided any common physical descriptors—age, height, weight, hair color, facial hair, facial features, eye color, complexion, footwear, or headwear. The only description the victim provided to the original officer prior to viewing the alleged offenders at the show-up was very general; the victim described them as White or Hispanic,[5] wearing some combination of white T-shirts, shorts, and jeans.[6]

Although a hat belonging to one alleged offender and a wave cap belonging to another were photographed and submitted into evidence by the City police department, there is no direct evidence that any headwear was worn during the robbery by any offender, the victim did not identify the headwear as being dropped at the scene by the alleged offenders during the robbery, there is no suitable explanation as to their relevance or evidentiary value, and the headwear was not forensically tested for a connection to the alleged offenders. In fact, the defendants' counsel conceded in a letter that no records of DNA testing or other forensic analysis exist.

---

(Footnote 4 continued)

during the *Wade* hearing that he was struck twice on the head during the robbery with a piece of wood used as a weapon); *see also* [2].

[5] The 2005–2009 U.S. Census, *American Community Survey*, estimated the percentage of the population in the City that self-identifies their race as White is 58.3% and as Hispanic or Latino of any race is 76.4%. Those in the City who specifically self-identify as Puerto Rican comprise 28.1% of the population, which is the largest Hispanic/Latino subgroup in the City.

[6] *See* U.S. v. De Jesus-Rios, 990 F. 2d 672, 677–678 (1st Cir. 1993) (identification was held unreliable because the witness described the defendant as White and 5′2″ although the defendant actually had light brown skin and was 5′6″); Raheem v. Kelly, 257 F. 3d 122, 139 (2nd Cir. 2001) (identification was held unreliable because witness did not describe any distinctive features and testified the shooter "looked like any other person who was dressed real neat"); Cossel v. Miller, 229 F. 3d 649, 655–656 (7th Cir. 2000) (identification was held unreliable because the witness described the offender as no taller than 6′0″ and 140–150 pounds, when the defendant was actually 6′3″ and weighed 215–220 pounds at time of the attack); Tomlin v. Myers, 30 F. 3d 1235, 1241–1242 (9th Cir. 1994) (identification was held unreliable because the witness described the offender as being 5′6″–5′8″ tall with heavy build and "afro" hair when defendant was actually 6′0″ tall, thin, and had straight, shoulder-length hair); Thigpen v. Cory. 804 F. 2d 893, 896–897 (6th Cir. 1986) (identification was held unreliable because victim only briefly viewed offender once during the robbery).

*The level of certainty demonstrated by the witness at the confrontation.* The victim was equivocal about his identification. The supporting detective who was on-scene during the show-up procedure testified at deposition that she asked the victim how certain he was about the third alleged offender: "I asked him—he told me he was sure about two, positive about two. And the third one he told me he only remembered his physical stature and told me he could possibly remember him because he was chasing him, but he wasn't sure. He wasn't sure about his face, only his physical build." In her deposition, she reiterated what the victim said when asked whether he could positively identify all three men: "The victim told me that he positively recognized two people and that the third one he only saw his physical stature and that he may have seen him running away but he wasn't sure." The victim was not certain the day of the show-up or two days later when he was presented with a photographic display of the alleged offenders by the City's detectives, and his in-court identification was inconsistent with his identification at the scene.

The original responding officer testified at deposition that he did not recall asking the victim: (1) whether or not he could identify the alleged offenders; (2) whether or not he got a good look at the alleged offenders; and (3) just how confident he was about the identification he was making, which are standard questions that should be asked during a robbery investigation. Furthermore, as to the level of confidence in the identification expressed by the victim, the lead robbery investigator testified at deposition "we don't—we don't ask, 'How sure are you'? It's what response that he gives gets put into the report there." His position on confirming the witnesses' level of certainty is inconsistent with accepted practices on eyewitness identification[7] and contrary to the established procedural law standard (*Neil v. Biggers*), which dictates police officers are to state the witnesses' degree of certainty for future reference. Additionally, (1) the victim never made any affirmative statements demonstrating his certainty during the show-up procedure; (2) the victim subsequently failed to identify the third offender during a photograph display conducted by City detectives two days after the incident; and (3) the victim's in-court identification was not absolute.[8]

Furthermore, the lead investigator testified at deposition that it was common to conduct a show-up in which more than one alleged offender is presented to the witness at the same time and he acknowledged that he did not know the policy and procedure on show-up identifications as it existed when this crime occurred. His appeal to common practice—the fact that show-up identifications were conducted involving multiple alleged offenders standing together—does not render the practice reasonable, or the results justified. This suggests skill-based errors and routine violations. The routine nature of show-up violations that he testified to implicates the supervisory chain, as well as informal work around processes developed by the officers that deviate from accepted industry practices.

---

[7] *See* National Institute of Justice 1999, [3] at 27.

[8] This testimony was derived from the motion to suppress transcript.

*The length of time between the crime and the confrontation.* The show-up between the victim and the alleged offenders took place on the same afternoon as the robbery outside a multi-family house in the City, which is approximately 0.4 miles east of the primary crime scene.[9] The temporal and physical proximities to the primary crime scene are reasonable in which to conduct a show-up identification procedure and do not implicate due process.

## 6.1.2 Internal and External Pressure for Results Due to Rising Crime

Although not explicitly stated and no direct evidence exists, there is indirect evidence that the City police department may have been facing internal (administrative) and external (community) pressure for enforcement action because of the rising crime rate. The evidence did not arise through anything the plaintiffs alleged but through the defendants' own expert witness during the civil proceedings, who alluded in his report to the magnitude of the crime problem, particularly violent crime facing the City in 2007:

> "According to [published crime reports] for the year 2007, the violent crime rate in the [City] more than tripled that of the previous year 2006. This substantial jump in the [City's] crime rate is particularly well exemplified by the following: (1) the number of robberies jumped from 26 in 2006 to 116 in 2007; (2) the overall crime rate jumped from 17.0 per 1,000 persons in 2006 to 27.3 per 1,000 persons in 2007; (3) the number of actual violent crimes jumped from 75 in 2006 to 216 in 2007; (4) there were a total of 775 motor vehicle thefts reported in City in 2007, five for every police officer employed by the City [p. 6]...*The [City] has a substantial crime problem. In fact, the violent crime rate in the [City] more than tripled in the twelve months preceding this incident* [emphasis mine]. As such, the agency was compelled to ensure that its business processes reflected those that are the most effective and efficient in order to fulfill their responsibility to provide for public safety [p. 22]."

When crime rises, the due process perspective of the criminal justice process may give way to the crime control perspective, where police officers may "bend the rules" and may not comply with constitutional safeguards.[10] The concurrent rise in crime inherently translates into increased workload for patrol officers and

---

[9] The distance between the primary crime scene and the multi-family house where all three alleged offenders were located was measured using Google Maps© pedestrian mode.

[10] *See* Refs. [4, 5] (discussing how constitutional restrictions become more suspect in the face of community pressure to crackdown on crime; anyone considered "disorderly" is by definition beyond a respectable citizen and perhaps does not deserve the same level of protections against state authority, at 11); Ref. [6] (discussing the link between unconstitutional searches and the municipality's "war on drugs" rhetoric); Mills v. District of Columbia, 571 F.3d 1304 (D.C. Cir. 2009) (holding roadblocks erected by the Washington, D.C., Metropolitan Police Department in the face of increasing crime, whose "primary purpose" is to "serve the general interest in crime control," is unconstitutional, which implies that rising crime rates alone are not sufficient to justify such a reaction from the police who cast their net wider to see who they might catch in their effort to reduce crime).

detectives and typically brings production pressure to solve cases and reduce the crime rate.[11] Despite the defense expert's opinion about the police department's "business practices [being]…most effective and efficient…," the police department had no "business practice" whatsoever in the form of a policy on show-up procedures and criminal investigations prior to this incident, nor did the agency make it their business to conduct periodic in-service training on show-up procedures.

## 6.1.3 Unsafe Supervision

A City police lieutenant—mid-level manager—was the highest-ranking officer at the scene of the incident and testified at deposition that he was acting as the "street supervisor." The lieutenant has the authority and responsibility to direct the preliminary investigation by assigning resources to ensure that appropriate police action is taken, providing subordinate personnel with advice and technical assistance, as well as reviewing his subordinates' work to ensure that proper procedures are followed and reasonable standards of workmanship are maintained.[12] By delegating assignments to his subordinates, the lieutenant is initiating and ensuring specific actions that are taken to achieve desired police objectives. In doing so, he also delegates the authority to his subordinates to accomplish those objectives, but he does not delegate responsibility; he remains accountable for his actions and those of his subordinates.[13]

In addition to formal authority bestowed by his rank, the lieutenant also testified that he had experience supervising criminal investigations and directing subordinate personnel from his previous assignment as a sergeant in the City police

---

[11] *See* Packer [7] (discussing the ever-present competing interests of crime control [production] and due process [safety]); *see also* Ref. [8] (discussing public pressure on the President and Congress to pass crime control legislation); Ref. [9] (discussing the internal and external pressure to improve performance in the homicide investigation process); Ref. [10] (discussing how external pressure and activism are applied to a police agency to have police policies and practices added to the City agenda); Ref. [11] (where police chiefs responded via survey that they were pressured by the mayor (28%), City council members (29%) and business leaders (6%) for arrest or enforcement action; the findings revealed political pressure contributed significantly to police chiefs' non-survival); *Rampart Reconsidered: The Search for Real Reform Seven Years Later*, (no date), at 27 (discussing how "…political pressure to reduce [spiraling crime] produced a distorted focus on [performance] numbers that fueled tendencies to use 'any means necessary'" and reinforce a cultural disposition of "warrior policing" in the Los Angeles Police Department. Retrieved on April 3, 2012 from http://www.lapdonline.org/assets/pdf/Rampart%20Reconsidered -Full%20Report.pdf).

[12] The lieutenant's job responsibilities are defined by the state's department of civil service.

[13] *See generally* Iannone and Schroeder, Lombardo & Stollo [12, 13].

department's detective division.[14] There are several acts and omissions[15] regarding on-scene supervision that are not consistent with agency policies, nor are they consistent with reasonable, accepted, and customary industry standards for supervising a preliminary investigation during field operations,[16] which likely influenced the unsafe act.

*Assembling the show-up procedure.* As the show-up administrator, the lieutenant improperly orchestrated the simultaneous show-up.[17] Allowing a victim to view multiple alleged offenders simultaneously instead of sequentially violates the logic of the state Attorney General's policy on conducting photographic and live line up procedures, as well as the tenets of *Neil v. Biggers*. A sequential showing is intended to reduce suggestibility, which produces a more reliable identification.[18] Despite the lieutenant's advanced investigative training, his previous assignment as a sergeant in the City detective division, and his current rank he testified that he did not give any officers at the scene instructions for conducting the show-up procedure, he was not familiar with the common practice of conducting show-ups and he was not aware of whether it was unusual to conduct a show-up with multiple suspects.

*Preserving the crime scene.* Crime scene preservation is a long-standing basic principle of U.S. policing that is a matter of investigative integrity. One of the first official actions that should have been taken by the first responding officers was to isolate and preserve the scene to prevent contamination.[19] The City police department's policy states that the patrol supervisor is responsible for designating an officer to document access to the scene and to ensure that this officer denies unauthorized access to the scene. Direct evidence and proceeds are typically recovered at primary, secondary, and tertiary crime scenes. Preserving the crime

---

[14] The job responsibilities for a police sergeant are defined by the state's department of civil service.

[15] The distinction between an act and an omission should be thought of this way: an act is overt positive action, and an omission is overt negative action. Both acts (taking the wrong course of action) and omissions (failing to take the correct course of action) can arise from conditions such as preoccupation, deliberateness, ignorance, laziness, inattention, or forgetfulness that may be facilitated by fatigue, medical, pharmacological condition, or bias. In the case of police officers, they are duty bound to act so their omissions are tantamount to acts.

[16] *See* citations Adams [14], Hale [15], International Association of Chiefs of Police [16], Giacalone [17], Lyman [18], Sonne [19], National Institute of Justice [20], Swanson et al. [21], Geberth [22] and Hess and Orthmann [23].

[17] *See* National Institute of Justice [3].

[18] *See* Ref. [24] (explaining that when the actual offender is absent, the witness tends to identify an innocent person who looks more like the offender than the other individuals in the lineup).

[19] *See generally* citations at Adams [14], Hale [15], International Association of Chiefs of Police [16], Giacalone [17], Lyman [18], Sonne [19], National Institute of Justice [20], Swanson et al. [21], Geberth [22] and Hess and Orthmann [23]; (one City police department policy on preserving the crime scene vests the officer conducting the preliminary investigation with such responsibility. A separate City police policy on collecting, preserving, and processing evidence states "The initial officer to arrive at the scene of a crime, accident, or incident will be responsible for securing the scene to preserve any evidence that may be present").

scene enables investigators to document the scene in its natural state as it existed at the time of the crime and to collect items of evidentiary value that leads to successful prosecution.

There are no data to indicate that the primary crime scene, the secondary crime scene (the first-floor and basement apartments at the multi-family house), and the tertiary crime scene (the alleged offenders' vehicle) were secured with a crime scene barrier, and there are no data to indicate that a crime scene and log was prepared. In fact, defendant's counsel conceded in a letter to the plaintiffs that there are no records of a crime scene log. A series of crime scene photographs submitted by the crime scene technician show the outside of the primary crime scene and secondary crime scene. None of the photographs show a crime scene barrier that was erected protecting them from unauthorized entry.

As such, direct evidence and proceeds that should have been collected may have been lost, destroyed, or overlooked; it is this independent evidence that should have been collected in an effort to establish the corpus of the crime and to connect the alleged offenders to the crime. Moreover, the tertiary crime scene (the alleged offenders' vehicle) was not photographed in its original state before it was impounded; the vehicle should have been photographed where it was discovered before it was removed, and the area beneath the vehicle should have been searched for evidence and proceeds following its removal. The photographs of the vehicle were not taken until the vehicle reached the impound facility, and there are no data to support that the vehicle had to be removed prior to being photographed. The original responding officer testified at deposition that when he encountered the alleged offenders' vehicle, he never touched it to determine whether it was hot, which would support a reasonable inference that the engine was recently running and may have been used by the offenders. The vehicle allegedly used by the offenders became central to the preliminary investigation; the vehicle's license plate registration led the officers to the multi-family house, where they discovered the registered owner was friendly with the two accomplices who were found inside her apartment and who were identified by the victim, yet the police did not collect any evidence connecting the alleged offenders to the vehicle or to the robbery.

In addition, the primary crime scene was never sketched[20] to depict the pertinent details of the assault and robbery, and there are no official documents that reveal the details necessary to support the corpus of the crime. Although a widely accepted industry standard, a standard set by the City police department's policy, and given the lieutenant's past experience as a detective division supervisor, the lieutenant testified at deposition that creating a sketch of the crime scene is not part of crime scene processing.

Lastly, the victim testified at the *Wade* hearing that the alleged offenders threw the computer's keyboard and screen on him during the robbery and they tried to open the "money box" (cash register). The fact that one of the alleged offenders threw the computer's keyboard and screen on him during the robbery was never

---

[20] *See* Giacalone [17] at 46–47; Lyman [18], at 73–78.

documented by a police officer at the scene; the first time it arose was the *Wade* hearing.

In a series of crime scene photographs submitted by the City police department as evidence, the keyboard and screen are shown sitting atop the customer counter and are not on the floor as if they had been thrown or disconnected in any way. The victim also testified that the alleged offenders tried to open the "money box," which is contradicted by the photographs.[21] This is consistent with the crime scene having been altered or cleaned by someone, but there is no indication from the crime scene technician's official report that the crime scene was altered or cleaned by the victim or anyone else prior to the photographs being taken. Also, the same crime scene photographs that the City police are relying on to prove the corpus of the crime do not show the weapon. These are indications that the crime scene was contaminated.[22]

*Maintaining the inner perimeter.* There are three entrances to the secondary crime scene, the front, the side, and the rear.[23] The rear entrance was covered by the original responding officer, and the front entrance was covered by two other officers. This left the side entrance uncovered, where someone could have entered or exited unseen. There are no data to support that an inner perimeter was set up around the house to contain the scene, which is a long-standing basic principle of U.S. policing for preserving a crime scene and containing alleged offenders. In addition, once the officers entered the house, there is no documentation that the second-floor area was searched or secured, where someone could have been hiding. There is also no documentation showing who controlled the front and rear entrances after the police officers left their position to enter the house.

*Collecting corroborating evidence.* Collecting and marking evidence recovered from a crime scene is a long-standing basic principle of U.S. policing that is extremely important to the ensuing investigation and is a process connected to crime scene preservation.[24] Direct evidence and proceeds are typically recovered at the primary and secondary crime scenes the same day as the incident, which is intended to corroborate facts and support the corpus of the crime. If the crime scene cannot be processed in a single day, then the scene should be secured with police officers until the next day when the search resumes. An unsecured crime scene leads to contamination, which compromises the integrity of the scene and the eventual prosecution.

---

[21] The photographs show that the cash register was not disturbed in any way as though someone had tried to open it.

[22] *See generally* citations at Adams [14], Hale [15], International Association of Chiefs of Police [16], Giacalone [17], Lyman [18], Sonne [19], National Institute of Justice [20], Swanson et al. [21], Geberth [22] and Hess and Orthmann [23].

[23] This was confirmed by the audio recorded interview of the basement apartment's occupant by a County prosecutor's office investigator. Also, photographs submitted by the City police confirm the front, side, and rear entrances of the house.

[24] *See* Adams [14], at 29, 322–323; Giacolone [17], at 37–56; Hale [15], at 20–22; International Association of Chiefs of Police [16], at 74–78; Lyman [18], at. 25–49; Swanson, Chamelin and Territo [21], at 39–77.

A detective from the City police department responded as the crime scene technician who processed the primary crime scene; however, his report is short, vague, and unspecific as to what he processed, if anything, beyond taking photographs and searching for latent fingerprints. There are no data to indicate that he processed the scene in a thorough manner consistent with accepted police practice[25] to support the impending prosecution, for example, he failed to

1. Describe the physical characteristics and appearance of the scene from his perspective;
2. Recover the weapon;
3. Indicate the specific items or areas from which he tried to lift latent fingerprints;
4. Sketch the scene;[26]
5. Erect a crime scene barrier;
6. Indicate whether he recovered any evidence from the primary crime scene or from the tertiary crime scene;
7. Indicate whether he searched the tertiary crime scene for latent fingerprints as well as having photographed it;
8. Process the multi-family house, the secondary crime scene, where the alleged offenders were located;
9. Identify who secured the primary crime scene before his arrival, or whether someone removed the crime scene barrier;
10. Indicate what actions were taken by other officers before his arrival at the primary crime scene, nor did he reference any reports submitted by other officers who may have taken action at the primary crime scene;
11. Identify the other personnel at the scene;
12. Identify the equipment used to process the scenes;
13. Indicate whether measurements were taken;[27]

---

[25] *See* Lyman, Adams [14], Hale [15], International Association of Chiefs of Police [16], Giacalone [17], Lyman [18], Sonne [19], National Institute of Justice [20], Swanson et al. [21], Geberth [22] and Hess and Orthmann [23]; CALEA standard 83.2.6 (*A written directive governs the preparation of a report by the person who processes a crime/traffic collision scene*) mandating written directives for preparing investigation reports; National Institute of Justice, 20 (processing the crime scene is also defined by the City police department's policy on crime scene preservation and evidence processing).

[26] Deposition testimony from an assistant prosecutor, an alibi witness and a supporting detective alleged the offenders were members of the Almighty Latin King and Queen Nation, an organized Hispanic gang, but no official documents or direct evidence was offered. Although sketching the scene is discretionary according to the City police department's policy, an armed robbery scene involving an assault and alleged gang members warrants a crime scene sketch to augment the prosecution.

[27] The crime scene technician submitted four photographs that show an unidentified person inside the crime scene using a tape measure to measure what appears to be the height and width of the customer counter. The measurements are unreadable, they are not referenced anywhere in his report narrative, there is no description of what the photographs are intended to explain and is not possible to identify if the photograph actually belongs to this investigation.

14. Indicate whether any items were disturbed during the robbery;
15. Indicate what measures he took to minimize contaminating the crime scene by himself and other personnel at the scene; and
16. Conclude whether the alleged offenders were connected to the tertiary crime scene even though the alleged offenders reportedly got out of the vehicle.

Moreover, as per the City police department's policy on collecting, preserving, and processing evidence, the crime scene technician had available to him the County prosecutor's crime scene unit to assist at the crime scene, but he did not make the request. The City police department's policy on collecting evidence vests the assigned officer with responsibility for requesting a detective to "...arrange for and supervise the search for the collection of physical evidence which might serve to further the criminal investigation." There are no data to indicate this occurred; consequently, there is no corroborating physical evidence, and the weapon was not recovered and entered into evidence until September 2008 by the County prosecutor's office, by that time the scene was contaminated.

*Searching the crime scene.* There were four crime scenes: (1) the primary scene; (2) the secondary scene—second-floor apartment; (3) the secondary scene—basement apartment; and (4) the tertiary scene—parked vehicle. The lead investigator testified at deposition that he never conducted any subsequent searches for evidence or proceeds of the crime at the secondary crime scene the day of the robbery or any other day, particularly the second-floor apartment, which is where two of the three alleged offenders were discovered (e.g., one alleged offender's clothing that matched the victim's description was discovered outside the shower in the bathroom, but was never photographed, positively identified by the victim, or collected as evidence). Later in his deposition, he changed his position and testified that he did search the second-floor apartment, but did not recover anything and that a supporting detective helped him search the apartment; that supporting detective testified at deposition that she did not search the second-floor apartment or any other apartment at the secondary crime scene and that the lead investigator himself did not search the second-floor apartment. The original responding officer testified at deposition that he did not conduct a search of the rear of the secondary crime scene although he established a security position at the rear of the building and that the second responding officer did not thoroughly search the second-floor apartment, where two of the alleged offenders were located. The second responding officer testified at deposition that he did not search all the closets, under the bed, under anything in the kitchen and the hallway area, spaces that could have easily concealed a person, evidence, or proceeds of the crime.

A fundamental aspect of investigation following a robbery is to immediately search for evidence, proceeds of the crime, and additional offenders. Neither the City police nor the County prosecutor's office applied for a search warrant or obtained written consent to search the second-floor apartment (secondary crime scene), the alleged offender's vehicle (tertiary crime scene), or the basement apartment (secondary crime scene) for corroborating evidence. It is evident that both agencies believed that there was a nexus between the suspects, the vehicle, and both apartments since (1) the alleged offenders were discovered inside the second-floor apartment; (2) all three alleged offenders were arrested for the robbery; (3) the police interviewed the female occupant of the second-floor apartment and the male occupant of the basement apartment who offered alibis for two of the alleged offenders; (4) witnesses told City police that the alleged offenders were seen near the vehicle (the tertiary crime scene), which was subsequently impounded and photographed by police; and (5) a male witness indicated that he saw the three alleged offenders run inside the multi-family house.

Although there is a conflicting testimony about whom and whether a search was conducted, there are no data to indicate that written consent to search was obtained and there are no search warrants for the target location. In fact, defendant's counsel conceded in a letter to the plaintiffs that there are no records of written consent to search. To bolster their case and overcome their legal burden of proof, before undertaking the search, the police should have sought written consent instead of relying on verbal consent.

*Canvassing the neighborhood.* A neighborhood canvass is intended to uncover witnesses and evidence of a crime and should be as thorough as possible.[28] The City police department's policy on neighborhood canvassing states that officers will be assigned to conduct the canvass as soon as possible. The authority to assign the officers to conduct the canvass typically resides with a supervisor, although City's policy does not specify which supervisor; in this case, the supervisor was the lieutenant.

A neighborhood canvass is basic to the initial response, especially when the crime is fresh, before witnesses' memories fade, before any witnesses leave the scene, and before evidence is lost or destroyed. There is no documentation to support a neighborhood canvass was conducted. The 911 caller stated that the alleged offenders fled the store in the opposite direction from a gas station. This area is a commercial corridor; a commercial corridor in the City at 3 p.m. in July is likely to be busy with commuters, shoppers, and pedestrians who may have seen or heard the robbery. There is also a possibility that video surveillance records may exist from a nearby store or building that captured the alleged offenders entering the primary crime scene and/or escaping after the robbery.[29]

There is no documentation from the City police or the County prosecutor's office that any police officers or investigators conducted a neighborhood canvass along the escape route or in the area adjacent to the primary, secondary, and tertiary crime scenes to search for witnesses, co-conspirators, evidence, or proceeds of the robbery. The second responding officer testified at deposition that he "canvassed" the parking lot of a nearby apartment complex, while the crime was

---

[28] A canvass (or canvassing) is a systematic process of speaking to a broad array of people and visiting residential homes and businesses in an area where a crime has occurred, along the escape route where the crime occurred, and where offenders or evidence are located to uncover witnesses, offenders, evidence, and proceeds of the crime. *See* Ref. [25, 26]; Geberth [22], at 86; Giacolone [17], at 57–62, 92; Lyman [18], at 48.

[29] *See* Giacolone [17], at 59.

unfolding to search for secreted offenders. However, his testimony and his report reveal that he only made brief observations in the parking lot while patrolling at low speed, which is not a canvass; it is low-speed patrol. The officer did not canvass the apartment complex by getting out of his car, systematically speaking to people and recording pedigree information, or canvass inside any of the buildings.[30] Moreover, this officer was told by an anonymous female citizen that "...she observed three males matching the description run out from the yard...– towards [the apartment complex]," but this did not motivate him to search inside the building, request someone else do so, or notify his supervisor about what he was told.

In addition, this officer testified that there were vehicles parked on the street near the secondary crime, but there is no documentation from him, the lead detective, the supporting detective, or any other police officers that they copied license plates from the parked vehicles as part of the investigation. Copying license plates is a common investigative technique during a canvass, so the vehicle's registered owner can be interviewed to determine (1) whether they saw or heard anything; (2) whether they were involved; and (3) if they did not see or hear anything and they were not involved, to document negative statements.[31] This potentially valuable source of independent corroborating information was lost.

*Documenting and processing the primary, secondary, and tertiary crime scenes.* The lieutenant testified at deposition that while at the crime scene, he was the scene supervisor and he was in charge and responsible for ensuring "that the patrol officers are securing the scene." There are no official reports indicating that the primary, secondary, and tertiary crime scenes were properly secured, processed, and documented according to accepted industry standards or according to City police department policy. The City police department's policy also states that part of securing the crime scene is erecting a crime scene barrier and posting a police officer who initiates a crime scene log.[32] The lieutenant testified that it is not his responsibility to initiate a crime scene log; he did not ensure that a crime scene log was prepared, and he did not think that it was necessary.

---

[30] *See* McDevitt [26], at 171–172.

[31] *See* Giacalone [17], at 61; Lyman [18], at 34 (negative statements are used to confront a witness who subsequently comes forward after the investigation is completed to testify that they did see or hear something when they originally said they did not. When this occurs, the previous statement can be used to impeach the witness's credibility and to disclose the inconsistencies in his or her testimony).

[32] The City's policy states: "The initial officer will initiate the department's Crime Scene Log as soon as possible and record the name, badge #, agency, and the time anyone enters or leaves the scene. Unless otherwise advised by an officer of supervisory rank, no one is to be permitted access to the scene until the scene is turned over to the detective." A separate City policy directs the officers conducting the investigation to: "Initiate and maintain a chronological log recording the names, badges and commands of any police officers entering the crime scene. In addition, record the names, addresses, etc., of any civilians who may have to enter the crime scene. This log shall contain the time the persons entered and exited the crime scene...This log shall be initiated by the assigned uniformed officer and continued until conclusion of scene processing."

Not only this is factually incorrect, but also it is contrary to his job specification, which dictates that a police lieutenant in command of a crime scene is expected to direct subordinate officers by delegating specific aspects of the preliminary investigation such as securing the crime scene and preparing a crime scene log. The lieutenant testified that (1) he did not assign someone to secure or search the second-floor apartment (secondary crime scene); (2) he did not consult with the detectives on-scene; (3) he did not assign someone to secure the basement apartment (secondary crime scene); (4) he did not assign someone to secure the primary crime scene; and (5) he did not assign someone to secure the alleged offender's vehicle (tertiary crime scene).

The lieutenant also testified at deposition that City detectives have their own supervisory staff. There are no reports indicating that the lieutenant summoned a detective supervisor to the scene to supervise the ensuing follow-up investigation. In the absence of a detective supervisor—which is the case in this matter—personnel at the scene are required to follow instructions from the lieutenant. There are no reports indicating that the lieutenant issued instructions to secure and process the primary, secondary, and tertiary crime scenes consistent with the City police department's policy, despite that the policy is clear about these activities, that it comports well with accepted industry practice for command and control of a crime scene[33] and that it provides adequate instruction about being in command at the scene.[34]

Lastly, initiating a search for evidence and proceeds of the crime and documenting the results associated with these activities are basic principles of a preliminary investigation.[35] The lieutenant testified at deposition that securing the crime scene and making sure that evidence is secured are two tasks that need to be

---

[33] The City's policy states: "Upon arrival, the duty detective will assume control of the scene. Although the street supervisor will maintain operational control of the scene and personnel present as per Rule & Regulation...the duty detective will be responsible for the decisions made regarding processing of the scene as per Rule and Regulation...The duty detective will carry out tasks assigned by the street supervisor that are in keeping with the detective's role in the investigation and the supervisor's responsibilities under Rule and Regulation...To assume command and direction of police personnel to assure the most efficient accomplishment of the police task. If a detective supervisor responds he will relieve the street supervisor as per Rule and Regulation...so that the street supervisor can return to their general patrol supervisory functions."

[34] The City's policy states: "*Command of the Scene*. The Watch Commander shall assign a Patrol Division supervisor to respond to the scene of a homicide, other serious crime or incident, or catastrophic event. RESPONSIBILITIES: The assigned patrol supervisor shall, upon arrival, assume command of the crime/incident scene, and shall implement crime scene precautions as outlined in the previous section for initial responding officers. The assigned superior officer shall also: (1) Assist the Detective personnel; (2) Oversee, and be held strictly accountable for, the actions of uniformed personnel at the scene, and for all non-uniformed personnel until the arrival of a Detective Supervisor; (3) Not leave the scene until properly relieved by a Detective Supervisor; (4) Once relieved, the Detective Supervisor will assume command of the crime/incident scene and be accountable for all uniformed and non-uniformed police personnel at the scene."

[35] *See* Lyman & National Institute of Justice [18, 20].

accomplished at a crime scene. By virtue of his rank and authority, he was responsible for initiating a crime scene search by delegating specific tasks to the officers, but he failed to do so. Consequently, evidence and proceeds of the robbery may have been lost, destroyed, or overlooked. In fact, the weapon used in the crime was not recovered until nearly 14 months after the incident by the County prosecutor's office, not by the City police department. By that time, the scene was contaminated.

*Documenting sworn statements from some witnesses and others in a timely manner.* There are no reports indicating that statements were taken from witnesses the day of the incident or that the witnesses were kept separate to avoid discussing the event with each other. The lieutenant testified that other than the victim, he was not aware of other witnesses being interviewed and he did not assign anyone to interview them. In fact (1) a sworn statement was never taken from one male witness who reportedly saw three people run inside the multi-family house; (2) a sworn statement was never taken from the anonymous witness who identified the alleged offenders' vehicle; (3) a sworn statement was never taken from a male who was discovered inside the primary crime scene with the victim at the time of the incident[36]; and (4) sworn statements were not taken from the second-floor occupant or the basement occupant (the alibi witnesses) until nearly 3 months after the incident in October 2007.

Moreover, the lieutenant testified that he did not speak to any witnesses, he did not speak to any neighbors, and he did not see anyone speaking to any witnesses. There are no reports indicating that the witnesses were not available for an interview on the day of the incident, and there are no reports indicating why the interviews were delayed. In addition, the City police unsuccessfully attempted to interrogate the third alleged offender (plaintiff) on the day of the event before they collected corroborating information and evidence from other witnesses about the incident. This placed the police at a tactical disadvantage since they were not forearmed with facts and information, which they could have used to confront the alleged offender as they tried to corroborate the physical evidence and look for inconsistencies between his statements and the evidence.

Based on his job specification, the lieutenant has the authority and responsibility to direct the crime scene, part of which is ensuring that all witnesses are detained, so their statements can be documented. Sworn statements from witnesses should have been documented the day of the incident before the third offender was interrogated and before any witnesses had the opportunity to talk to each other and to the alleged offenders. Statements also should have been taken from witnesses immediately following the incident, or as soon as practicable thereafter, while their memory and recollection of the event were fresh and before they had the opportunity to collude or swap stories, perceptions, or facts about the event, which

---

[36] None of the reports describe why the person was inside the store during the robbery or who he was [e.g., an employee, a visiting friend, a relative, a patron]. During deposition, a police officer said that he did not believe that the man could add anything to the investigation so he did not formally identify the man or take his statement, despite that the man heard the robbery occurred.

contaminates their independent recollection, a procedure recognized by City policy. The lieutenant testified at deposition that it is not his responsibility to ensure that statements are taken from witnesses, which is factually incorrect as per his job specification and contrary to agency policy and accepted industry practice.

*Interviewing the victim and examining him for injuries.* The lieutenant testified that he never spoke to the victim or anyone else about the case. By implication, he did not ask about the victim, he did not know whether the victim was injured or impaired by alcohol, drugs, or prescription medication, and he did not speak to any officers about the victim's condition. Had he inquired then he may have learned that the victim was struck twice in the head with a wooden board and may have needed medical treatment. Given the strike to the head, the victim's physical ability to identify the alleged offenders is questionable and his injury was not photodocumented as a matter of evidence.

Similarly, the second responding officer who wrote the original incident report testified that he did not speak to the victim at all before he wrote his report. When the second responding officer failed to interview the victim, he too missed an opportunity to recover the weapon and to potentially preserve valuable trace evidence at the scene of the crime and to record intimate details of the incident. If the victim was treated for his injuries, then the police officers could have documented the treating physician's medical opinion about his condition and whether the strikes to the head could have impaired his vision or memory.[37] Moreover, the victim's injuries should have been photographed as part of the investigation, regardless of whether or not they were visible; non-visible injuries (i.e., bruising) may not become evident until sometime later, and photographing the site of the injury documents the elements of the assault.[38] There is no documentation to suggest that these actions occurred.

*Assigning sufficient and appropriate personnel to support the preliminary investigation.* The lieutenant testified at deposition that part of his responsibility is to ensure "adequate manpower." There are no reports indicating that the lieutenant summoned additional personnel to the scene or that he summoned the detective division supervisors to the scene to ensure the preliminary investigation and the ensuing follow-up investigation had sufficient resources. In fact, he testified that he did not assign any other tasks. He also testified that he did not arrange for additional resources to help with witnesses interviews; more importantly, he testified that it was not his duty to do so. Given the tasks that needed to be completed (i.e., crime scene security and processing; evidence collection; victim and witness statements; interrogations; neighborhood canvass; victim medical treatment), the lieutenant should have delegated specific tasks to the officers and coordinated their

---

[37] *See* Sherley v. Seabold, 929 F.2d 272, 274–275 (6th Cir. 1991) (identification deemed unreliable because the victim suffered from memory loss); Ref. [27] (discussing the fallibility of human memory).

[38] *See* Lyman [18], at 325–326.

efforts and requested additional personnel and detective supervisors to respond to the scene, as necessary.[39]

Moreover, the lieutenant implied during deposition that once detectives arrive on the scene, he is no longer in charge of the preliminary investigation. This is factually incorrect and is contrary to his job specification and established City policy. The state's department of civil service—the organization that regulates certain aspects of policing in the state—does not recognize the status of "detective" as a formal rank that supersedes the rank of lieutenant at a crime scene,[40] and City policy states that the on-scene supervisor retains "operational control of the scene."

The lieutenant in charge of the scene also testified that he did not give any officers at the scene instructions for conducting the show-up procedure, he was not familiar with the common practice of conducting show-ups, and he was not aware of whether it was unusual to conduct a show-up with multiple suspects. This suggests both skill-based errors and decision errors. The skill-based errors reside in the lack of technical job knowledge, where industry-accepted investigation procedures were not followed; it reflects a poor-choice error, where an investigative detention[41] instead of an arrest was more appropriate given the facts known to him at the time.[42]

Despite these investigative errors, the lieutenant testified that he believed the City police officers had done their job and he was satisfied with their performance concerning this investigation. The lieutenant had been previously cautioned during a performance evaluation to "...ensure IR [incident reports] and arrest reports are

---

[39] Although there is no direct evidence to suggest that the crime scene was not adequately staffed, the number of tasks that needed to be completed that were not completed outnumbered the officers that were on scene.

[40] The lead investigator and the supporting detective testified at deposition that the lieutenant is in charge, and as detectives on the scene, they are bound to follow his orders.

[41] See Florida v. Bostic, 501 U.S. 429 (1991); Florida v. Royer, 460 U.S. 491, 497, 103 S.Ct. 1319, 1324 (1983); U.S. v. Drayton, 536 U.S. 194, 122 S.Ct. 2105, 2110 (2002).

[42] The facts weighing against the show-up that were known to the police beforehand included (1) the victim only saw the faces of two alleged offenders, not the third alleged offender; (2) the victim's failure to adequately describe or positively identify the third alleged offender; (3) the victim's vague and common clothing description; (4) the victim's tentative racial description; (5) the victim's failure to articulate any distinctive or unusual physical attributes; (6) the victim's failure to articulate any common physical descriptors beyond sex and race; (7) the victim was ordered to the floor and told "Don't look," he complied so he was no longer looking at the alleged offenders; (8) the lack of containment at the secondary crime scene, which potentially allowed other persons into and out of the building; (9) the incomplete search of the secondary crime scene for additional offenders, or evidence and proceeds connecting the alleged offenders to the crime; (10) the failure to search the apartment building, where an unidentified female citizen told the second responding officer that she observed three males matching the description run inside; (11) the unsupported and tenuous connection between the alleged offenders and the vehicle [the tertiary crime scene]; (12) the lack of corroborating evidence beyond the clothing, sex, and racial description; (13) the lack of corroborating witness identification, despite one male witness seeing three people run inside the multi-family house and one witness seeing three people associated with the alleged offenders' vehicle.

in compliance with our arrests and procedures," which suggests that the reports he authored or those he reviewed at one time were out of compliance. The investigative reports submitted by the officers in this case lack details and specificity and are not consistent with accepted industry standards for police report writing.[43] Furthermore, the lieutenant testified that he was previously reprimanded for failing to supervise.[44]

## 6.2 Preconditions for Unsafe Acts

The police response to a crime, beginning with the initial report and the actions of the original arriving officers, is the first opportunity to confirm that a crime has been committed, identify and apprehend the alleged offender, preserve the crime scene, collect evidence, secure witnesses, and build the prosecution's case.[45] It is also an opportunity to dispel the original report as a hoax or at least something different than the original report. There are several acts and omissions committed during the preliminary investigation that do not comport with accepted industry standards and suggest that the investigation was inadequate, which likely facilitated the misidentification.

*Preserving the original* 911 *call transaction.* The original 911 call is an important aspect of the investigation because it is a contemporaneous verbal record of the details of the event; this is something recognized by and articulated in City police policy. A transcribed written record of the 911 telephone call was prepared by an investigator from state's public defender's office. Telephone calls to police are the first opportunity to investigate the incident including identifying the offenders and are used as an investigative reference to recall details that may have been overlooked, to confirm or dispel what was said, by whom, when it was said and to establish an event timeline.[46] Neither the lead investigator nor his supervisor properly preserved the 911 call; therefore, it could not be referenced by investigators as support for the investigation. A transcription of the 911 call indicates that a robbery was reported, yet the 911 operator failed to probe the caller for common and crucial details about the incident, such as

---

[43]  See Ref. [28].

[44]  The lieutenant's praise and support for the officers suggest his loyalty to his peers over the profession. It also suggests his overconfidence in his subordinates' actions, despite the numerous errors that were committed; for similarities involving the loyalty ethic, values, and police culture see *City of New York, Commission to Investigate Allegations of Police Corruption and the Anti-Corruption Procedures of the Police Department*, at 51–69 (commonly known as the *Mollen Commission Report*, July 7, 1994, retrieved on May 7, 2012 from http://www.parc.info/client_files/Special%20Reports/4%20-%20Mollen%20Commission%20-%20NYPD.pdf.

[45]  *See* Lyman and National Institute of Justice [18, 20].

[46]  *See* National Institute of Justice [20].

1. Can anyone identify the offender(s)?
2. Can you describe the offenders? (followed by specific questions about age, sex, race, physical description, clothing description and unique characteristics);
3. Was there more than one offender?
4. Was anyone injured?
5. Was anyone assaulted?
6. Does anyone need emergency medical assistance?
7. Was a weapon involved? (if yes, then followed by specific questions about the weapon and its use);
8. Was a vehicle involved?
9. What was stolen?[47]

These are standard questions to ask during a reported robbery, which was confirmed through deposition testimony from a City police communication's supervisor, but there are no data to support this occurred. Moreover, the 911 communications operator allowed the complainant to terminate the call without asking for standard pedigree information (e.g., name, location, call-back number) and without telling them to remain at the scene to meet the responding police officers. If police told the complainant to meet the responding officers at the scene, then the officers could have documented their observations as part of the investigation.

*Accurately documenting the original computer-aided dispatch (CAD) report.* The CAD report is a contemporaneous written record of the event, which is used to capture the details of the incident and to make a permanent record. There are several inconsistencies between the official CAD report, the details provided by the original 911 caller, and the details provided by the original responding officer who was first to encounter the victim. The CAD report identifies (1) the alleged offenders "...observed with knives" and (2) one alleged offender as having a "ponytail." These facts were not conveyed by the original 911 caller,[48] and the original responding officer testified at deposition that he did not convey these details over the radio. There is no evidence that any other responding police officer provided this information, so the source is not known, which casts doubt on the accuracy and reliability of the data. None of the alleged offenders wore a ponytail hairstyle, which was confirmed by booking photographs, and knives were neither recovered nor mentioned by the victim (the victim testified that the offenders used a piece of wood as a weapon, not knives).

*Preserving the original police radio transmissions.* Radio transmissions between police officers in the field and the communications center are a contemporaneous verbal record of what is said among law enforcement personnel involved. There are

---

[47] These routine questions comport with the basic telecommunications' training curriculum offered by the state, specifically described in the overview of the police function and use of standard operating procedures; *see also* Adams [14], at 297; National Institute of Justice [20] at 13–14; Lyman [18], at 35–36 for a brief description of accepted industry practices on the police telecommunications function.

[48] These details do not appear in the 911 transcription.

no data to support that this incident was conveyed to the police officers in the field as an armed robbery; the second responding officer testified that he was never aware that a weapon was involved or that the alleged offenders had their faces covered or that anyone wore a ponytail; the crime scene technician wrote in his report that he was notified that the crime was a "burglary," not a robbery, adding to their confusion. Radio transmissions like telephone calls are used as an investigative reference to recall specific details, confirm or dispel what was said, by whom, when it was said, and to establish an event timeline. Neither the lead investigator nor his supervisor properly preserved the radio transmissions; therefore, they were not available to investigators as reference material during the investigation.

The radio transmissions also could not be reviewed to verify the offenders' description or any other facts that were transmitted to help corroborate the incident. In his deposition, the second responding officer testified to the very limited description that was broadcasted over the radio by the original responding officer as the incident was unfolding.

*Preserving the victim's statement, vouchering evidence, and taking statements from other witnesses.* Victim and witness statements are part of the preliminary investigation and help corroborate details of the alleged crime.[49] The victim's sworn statement of how the crime occurred is one of the most critical elements of a thorough and accurate investigation because it is the victim who often activates the criminal justice apparatus and whose veracity is typically not in question. The crime victim also symbolizes larger society that the criminal law serves to protect and who subjects himself or herself to penalties for activating the criminal justice system improperly.

The supporting detective testified that she obtained a recorded video statement from the victim; however, the video was lost or destroyed, and there is no evidence the statement actually ever existed, such as a vouchered property report. The lead investigator was reprimanded for failing to properly place the video statements of two of the alleged offenders into evidence.[50] In addition, sworn statements were not taken from witnesses during the preliminary investigation, including (1) the male who was discovered inside the primary crime scene when the crime occurred; (2) the male witness who saw three people run inside the multi-family house; (3) the anonymous eyewitness who told the original responding officer about the parked vehicle; and (4) the complainants who originally called 911 to report the robbery.

## 6.3 Unsafe Acts

The proximate cause of the accident was effecting an arrest based on the victim's equivocal identification during the show-up in the absence of corroborating evidence to support the identification. Probable cause to arrest does not exist on

---

[49] *See* Lyman [18]. National Institute of Justice [20].

[50] The City police issued the lieutenant an oral reprimand in August 2010.

hunch, rumor, or reasonable suspicion; it is fact based and is tested against the totality of the circumstances by examining all of the facts and circumstances known to a police officer when they are investigating a crime.[51] When the facts are equivocal, they never ripen into probable cause; when probable cause does not exist, a police officer cannot legally effect an arrest.

When all three alleged offenders were presented simultaneously instead of sequentially, the victim identified all three as being involved. This is the linchpin of the preliminary investigation; it was at this moment the police officers believed that they had probable cause to arrest and they had been focusing their attention and investigative techniques on the information that tended to support the expected or desired result at that time (i.e., arresting the offenders). However, not only did the simultaneous presentation unduly influence the victim's identification, but also the victim's statement about his certainty toward the plaintiff being involved was equivocal, an indicator of impending danger that should have served as a caution signpost. As further evidence of the victim's uncertainty, he provided a sworn declaration about what transpired between him and the police officers on the scene:

"...I only saw the faces of two of the three men...The third man stood by the door to my store. He had a white piece of cloth covering his face the entire time, so I was never able to see his face. While we were in the [police] car, I told the officer that I had only seen the faces of two of the three men who robbed my store [p. 1]...When we drove past [the house], I told the police officer that 'esos son los tres' or 'esos los tres son' ["these are the three"] I said this because I recognized the faces of two of the men as the robbers. I did not recognize the third person who was standing with them outside [the house]. I told the police officer that I was not sure about the identity of the third person because I never saw the third robber's face. I repeated that I had only seen the faces of two of the three men who robbed me...I was careful to tell the police officer that I was not sure about the identity of the third person because I had only seen the faces of two of the three robbers...Later that day I went to the police station, where I was interviewed by a different police officer...During my interview, I told this officer that I had only seen the faces of two of the robbers...A couple days later, I was taken to the precinct to identify pictures of the men who had robbed me. When I arrived at the precinct I again told the police officer I spoke with that I had only seen the faces of two of the three men...Those were the two people whose faces I saw when they robbed my store, and who I saw in front of [the house]...When I was shown several pictures, I was not able to identify the man whose face had been covered during the robbery [p. 2]. While I wanted the people who robbed me to be found and punished, I never wanted to accuse anyone who I was not sure had committed the crime. I was always careful to tell every police officer and prosecutor that I spoke with that I had not seen the face of the third robber, and that I could not identify him with any certainty [p. 3]."

This case relied exclusively on the victim's identification. There was no corroborating physical or testimonial evidence collected during the preliminary investigation or follow-up investigation to support the impending prosecution,[52]

---

[51] Illinois v. Gates, 462 U.S. 213 (1983) (defining and describing the totality of the circumstances test and its use for determining whether probable causes exist).

[52] See Ref. [29] (discussing the importance of corroborating evidence to support a finding of probable cause); Lyman [18] at 48–49; [video evidence shows that the City police tried

which compounded the unlawful arrest. Although the accident occurred during the preliminary investigation, the follow-up investigation too was fraught with errors, predominantly omissions that indicate a careless investigation and lack of super-vision. Even after the arrest had been effected, there were so many failures the police missed an opportunity to stop the harm against the plaintiff from progressing as he was held in the county jail (see Table 3.2 for errors that occurred during the follow-up investigation).

## 6.4 The Prevalence of Acts and Omissions and the Failure Points

Whether the police act or fail to act when necessary can precipitate an accident. As such, it is important to unpack where acts and omissions may occur and who commits them to determine what presents the greatest risk. Although we are most interested in knowing where the risk lies before an accident occurs so it can be prevented, it is also important to know where the risk lies after the accident occurs to mitigate the effects. While the proximate cause of an accident may be either an act or omission, they may not be equally distributed, something previous research suggests.[53] Mapping the failure points begins by summarizing how the data are distributed.

### 6.4.1 Descriptive Analysis

Table 6.1 presents the descriptive statistics and metrics for the variables in the quantitative analysis ($n = 49$). The investigative stage, the error type, and the

---

(Footnote 52 continued)

unsuccessfully to obtain a confession from the plaintiff. Even if they had obtained a confession, an uncorroborated confession would not have been enough to sustain a conviction, *see* Warsz-ower v. United States, 312 U.S. 342 (1941); Isaacs v. United States, 159 U.S. 487 (1895); Miles v. United States, 103 U.S. 304, 311–312 (1880). Once the prosecution lost the *Wade* hearing, they did not have any corroborating evidence or judicially created remedies available to salvage the case, such as *inevitable discovery rule* Nix v. William, 467 U.S. 431 (1984); *attenuated taint doctrine* Nardone v. United States, 308 U.S. 338 (1939) and Wong Sun v. United States, 371 U.S. 471 (1963); or *independent source doctrine* Murray v. United States, 487 U.S. 533 (1988)].

[53] Jens Rasmussen, *What Can Be Learned from Human Errors Reports?* (In Duncan et al. [30]) (reviewed 200 significant event reports of nuclear power operations and found omissions accounted for 34% of "functionally isolated errors" and "other" omissions accounted for 9% of errors); Institute of Nuclear Power Operations, *An Analysis of Root Causes in* 1983 *Significant Event Reports, INPO* 84–027 (investigation revealed that 60% of "all human performance root causes" were from omissions and 64.5% of "maintenance-related activities" were from omission errors); Reason 1997 [31], at 95 (analyzed 122 maintenance lapses in a single airline carrier over three years and found 56% of errors were omissions).

**Table 6.1** Descriptive statistics

| Variables and metrics | N | % |
|---|---|---|
| *Investigative stage* | 49 | – |
| Preliminary = 1 | 25 | 51.0 |
| Follow-up = 0 | 24 | 49.0 |
| *Error type* | 49 | – |
| Act = 1 | 8 | 16.3 |
| Omission = 0 | 41 | 83.7 |
| *Agency role* | 49 | – |
| Management/supervision = 1 | 24 | 49.0 |
| Line function = 0 | 25 | 51.0 |

agency role are dichotomous. The investigative stage was nearly evenly split with 49% of the errors committed during the follow-up investigation and 51% of the errors committed during the preliminary investigation. Whether an act (16.3%) or omission (83.7%) was committed shows that omissions predominate. Errors committed by personnel in a management/supervisory role (49.0%) were slightly lower than errors committed by line personnel (51.0%).

Table 6.2 is the failure state profile, which was coded against James Reason's general failure types.[54] An important principle of assessing risk is that a disproportionate share of errors is likely concentrated in only a few categories of failure (known as the Pareto principle), which represent the riskiest types of errors.[55] This implies that diagnosing them, then, as a matter of efficiency, focusing corrective action on the few vital categories (intensiveness) instead of the trivial, many (extensiveness) may yield the greatest preventive benefits rather than focusing on the individual indicators, which only addresses symptoms not the underlying problem. This is not to suggest that all the failure categories do not deserve attention; it simply means applying resources where risk is greatest. Just two categories of failure (25.0%) contribute nearly eighty percent (77.5%) of the risk of an error occurring. Failing to observe proper procedures is the most frequently occurring error (71.4%), followed by poor-choice decisions (6.1%). The fact that agency-specific procedures for conducting show-ups and criminal investigations did not exist at the time of the incident does not alleviate the officers of their professional responsibility for care, but it is likely a strong contributing factor to the accident.

Table 6.3 is split into two panels, summarizing how acts and omissions are distributed. The upper panel summarizes the type of error based on the error stage leading to the accident (preliminary investigation), which is classified according to the organizational accident framework. There are twenty-four errors identified, where 20.0% of errors are acts of commission and 80.0% of errors are acts of omissions. Unsafe supervision clearly emerges as the leading error point (52.0%)

---

[54] Reason 1997 [31] at 132–135.

[55] *See* Ref. [32].

**Table 6.2** Failure state profile

| Failure categories | Errors | % of errors | Cumulative % of errors | Cumulative % of failure categories |
|---|---|---|---|---|
| Procedural error | 35 | 71.4 | 71.4 | 12.5 |
| Decision error—poor choice | 3 | 6.1 | 77.5 | 25.0 |
| Communication error | 2 | 4.1 | 81.6 | 37.5 |
| Defense error | 2 | 4.1 | 85.7 | 50.0 |
| Incompatible goals | 2 | 4.1 | 89.8 | 62.5 |
| Training error | 2 | 4.1 | 93.9 | 75.0 |
| Design error | 2 | 4.1 | 98.0 | 87.5 |
| Decision error—procedural | 1 | 2.0 | 100.0 | 100.0 |
| *Total* | 49 | 100.0 | | |

**Table 6.3** *Summary of Acts and Omissions*

*Summary of Acts and Omissions by Error Stage Leading to the Accident (n=25)*

| Error Stage | Error Type (%) | | Total |
|---|---|---|---|
| | Act | Omission | |
| Organizational Factors (n=6) | 8.0 | 16.0 | 24.0 |
| Unsafe Supervision (n=13) | 4.0 | 48.0 | 52.0 |
| Preconditions for Unsafe Acts (n=5) | 4.0 | 16.0 | 20.0 |
| Unsafe Acts (n=1) | 4.0 | 0.0 | 4.0 |
| Total | 20.0 | 80.0 | 100.0 |

*Summary of Acts and Omissions by Agency Role Following the Accident (n=24)*

| Agency Role | Error Type (%) | | Total |
|---|---|---|---|
| | Act | Omission | |
| Line function (lead Investigator) (n=22) | 8.3 | 83.3 | 91.7 |
| Management/supervision (investigative supervisor) (n=2) | 4.2 | 4.2 | 8.3 |
| Total | 12.5 | 87.5 | 100.0 |

followed by organizational factors (24.0%) and preconditions for unsafe acts (20.0%). This suggests at least two possibilities. First, the supervisor during the preliminary investigation may have been too "hands on," where he assumed too much active participation instead of an oversight role. He became embedded in the actual operation playing an active role that may have divided his attention at a time when he should have been coordinating, directing, and communicating among his subordinates to accomplish the work through them and to ensure that it was within accepted industry standards. Second, the supervisor may have been operating against pressure to arrest (i.e., production) given the escalating crime rate in an environment that did not supply him with the tools (i.e., operating policies and training) necessary to ensure due process (i.e., safety). There is direct evidence that the supervisor did not (1) have a show-up policy available; (2) delegate tasks to subordinates; and (3) communicate instructions to subordinates, which are supervisory functions aimed at leading, directing, and controlling personnel and which may have contributed to the accident and his poor decisions.

The lower panel shows the error type by agency role, following the accident (follow-up investigation). Acts of commission represented 12.5% of errors, and acts of omission represented for 87.5% of errors. The largest portion of errors (91.7%) resides with the lead investigator, followed by his supervisors (8.3%). This finding is consistent with the agency not having promulgated adequate policies specifying how criminal investigations should be undertaken and also implies a lack of knowledge for properly conducting criminal investigations. The findings here quantify support for the qualitative analysis that so few investigative tasks were completed that the impending prosecution was likely compromised and disconfirming evidence was not analyzed that might have freed the plaintiff sooner from county jail, thus reducing the harm to him. Although the investigative supervisor in this case was directly responsible for only 8% of the errors, the supervisory staff in general (i.e., chain of command) is indirectly implicated for failing to supervise the lead investigator's work product according to established standards. This raises the question: how could so many tasks go incomplete if supervisors were initiating action to ensure a thorough investigation all the while monitoring performance? It also raises important questions concerning the extent of the County prosecutor's oversight, specifically the prosecutor's ethical obligation to see that justice is done, not merely to seek convictions.[56]

## 6.4.2 Inferential Analysis

Because the data are categorical, chi square is the most appropriate procedure to examine differences between observed and expected values.[57] Measures of central tendency did not reveal any coding errors, and all scores fell within the specified numeric range. Since procedural errors account for the largest category of failure (Table 6.2), the first statistical procedure was to test the assumption that procedural errors occur at a constant rate. To examine this more closely, the data were dummy coded for the presence (1) or absence (0) of procedural errors, the null hypothesis being that each value will occur an equal number of times. A one-sample chi square test showed that the null hypothesis is rejected with a statistically significant deviation from the hypothesized values [$\chi^2(1) = 9.000$; $p < 0.003$], which confirms the descriptive analysis that procedural errors (71.4%) are more likely to occur than other types of errors (28.6%). Why the officers failed to follow proper procedures is not conclusively known, but a combination of factors such as forgetfulness, absent, unclear, and cumbersome policy provisions and lack of awareness may partly explain it. This is speculative, however,

---

[56] MODEL CODE OF PROFESSIONAL RESPONSIBILITY EC 7–13 (2004) (stating that the prosecutor's "...duty is to seek justice, not merely convict"); Berger v. United States, 295 U.S. 78, 88 (1935) (emphasizing "[the prosecution's] interest, therefore, in a criminal prosecution is not that it shall win a case, but that justice shall be done").

[57] See Ref. [33].

observing proper procedures and the link between executing proper procedures and proper tactics is a mainstay of police training. This implies that if training beyond a minimal level did occur, then reinforcing procedures and tactics would have been emphasized to ensure the officers knew how to execute them properly. Moreover, the lieutenant who orchestrated the show-up testified that he did not know the proper procedures for conducting the show-up, which lends some evidence to this interpretation.

The next procedure was to test the assumption that acts and omissions occur at a constant rate. Previous studies suggest that there may be a difference between acts and omissions, and the descriptive analysis suggests that there is reason to believe this is so in this study. The null hypothesis is that acts of omission do not occur more frequently than acts of commission. Using a one-sample chi square test, we also reject the null hypothesis with a statistically significant difference between the type of error observed and what is expected, which is that omissions (87.5%) are more prevalent than acts (12.5%) $[\chi^2(1) = 22.224; p < 0.000]$. This is consistent with findings from other industries and implies that failures are likely to arise at various stages of life in an organization including planning, supervising, and executing a task. Part of the current focus is also to explore the relationship between the type of error committed (act or omission), the investigative stage (preliminary or follow-up), and the agency role (line or management/supervision). Since the data violate the chi square assumptions for small sample size (i.e., cells with expected counts less than five), Fisher's exact test was used. Although errors of omission are more prevalent than errors of commission, a statistically significant interaction was not found when comparing observed and expected values during the investigative stage [preliminary or follow-up; $\chi^2(1) = 0.504$; $p < 0.702$ FET] and based on agency role [management/supervision or line function, $\chi^2(1) = 0.699$; $p < 0.463$ FET].

Lastly, since procedural errors are more prevalent than other types of errors, it is important to explore the relationship between the type of error committed (procedural error or other), when the error occurs during an investigation (preliminary or follow-up stage), and who commits the error (line function or management/supervision) and estimating risk. The upper panel of Table 6.4 shows that procedural omissions accounted for 71.5% of the errors and other types of errors accounted for 28.5%. A statistically significant interaction was found $[\chi^2(1) = 5.954; p < 0.015]$ with a moderately strong effect size ($\Phi = 0.349$, $p < 0.015$), which suggests procedural omissions are more likely to occur during the preliminary investigation than during the follow-up investigation. This is a key finding since it is during the early onset of an accident, when circumstances and situations are unfolding (sometimes fraught with ambiguities), that interpretations are made and actions, reactions and overcorrection for events occur. It is also the point when police officers may be confronted with rapidly evolving circumstances and they are likely to forget or ignore procedures. It is also, however, the same point when procedures are most important since safety (for the officers and the citizens) is at stake. This is why scenario-based training that mimics real-world situations by placing the officers under situational stress and allowing them to

**Table 6.4** Cross-tabulation summaries and risk estimates

Investigative stage × Omission type

| Investigative stage | Omission type (%) | | |
| --- | --- | --- | --- |
| | Procedural | Other | Total |
| Preliminary ($n = 25$) | 28.6 | 22.4 | 51.0 |
| Follow-up ($n = 24$) | 42.9 | 6.1 | 49.0 |
| Total ($n = 49$) | 71.5 | 28.5 | 100.0 |
| $\chi^2(1) = 5.954$; $p < 0.015$; $\Phi = 0.349$, $p < 0.015$ | | | |

Agency role × Omission type

| Agency role | Omission type (%) | | |
| --- | --- | --- | --- |
| | Procedural | Other | Total |
| Management/supervision ($n = 24$) | 22.5 | 26.5 | 49.0 |
| Line ($n = 25$) | 49.0 | 2.0 | 51.0 |
| Total ($n = 49$) | 71.5 | 28.5 | 100.0 |
| $\chi^2(1) = 15.100$; $p < 0.000$; $\Phi = 0.555$, $p < 0.000$ | | | |

Risk estimate

| Error type | Agency role | Value | 95% CI | |
| --- | --- | --- | --- | --- |
| | | | Lower | Upper |
| (Procedural omissions/other) | Odds ratio for error type | 28.364 | 3.286 | 244.844 |
| | Line | 2.095 | 1.346 | 3.259 |
| | Management/supervision | 0.074 | 0.010 | 0.522 |
| | *Investigative stage* | | | |
| | Odds ratio for error type | 5.500 | 1.297 | 23.322 |
| | Preliminary | 1.562 | 1.070 | 2.282 |
| | Follow-up | 0.284 | 0.090 | 0.895 |

simulate a live exercise is likely to be the best way to compensate for the myriad circumstances that might arise.

The middle panel shows a relatively similar distribution as the upper panel between agency role and omission type. Procedural omissions accounted for the greatest proportion of errors, and line personnel committed slightly more errors (51%) than management/supervision personnel (49%). A statistically significant interaction was also found ($\chi^2(1) = 15.100$; $p < 0.000$) with a strong effect size ($\Phi = 0.555$, $p < 0.000$). This implies that procedural omissions at the line level are more likely to occur than at the management/supervisory level, which is expected given that line-level officers perform the majority of the work. However, since the distribution of errors between line personnel (51%) and management/supervision personnel (49%) is similar, this finding also implicates supervision insofar as supervisors are expected to monitor their subordinates' performance to ensure that workmanship meets accepted industry standards.

The lower panel shows the risk estimates of error probability. The relative risk of a procedural error being committed by line personnel is 2.1 times as likely as it is for management/supervision personnel (0.074) and 1.6 times as likely to occur during the preliminary investigation as during the follow-up investigation (0.284). This suggests that any training should be interactive involving line personnel and management/supervisors, so both groups can learn from the actions, reactions, and feedback of the other, particularly since supervision emerged as the leading error point accounting for 52% of the errors during the preliminary investigation (Table 6.3).

# References

1. Steblay, N. M. (1992). A meta-analytic review of the weapon focus effect. *Law and Human Behavior, 16*, 413–424.
2. Wells, G. L., & Murray, D. M. (1983). What can psychology say about the Neil v. Biggers criteria for judging eyewitness accuracy? *Journal of Applied Psychology, 68*(347), 349–350.
3. U.S. Department of Justice. (1999). *Eyewitness evidence: a guide for law enforcement* (p. 27). U.S.: National Institute of Justice.
4. Meares, T., & Kahan, D. (1999). *Urgent times: Policing and rights in inner city communities*. Boston: Beacon Press.
5. Saratn, A. (2009). New perspectives on crime and justice (Vol. 47). Greenwich: JAI Press.
6. Gould, J., & Mastrofski, S. (2004). Suspect searches: Assessing police behavior under the U.S. constitution. *Criminology & Public Policy, 3*, 315–362.
7. Packer, H. L. (1968). *The limits of the criminal sanction, Chapter 8, two models of criminal process* (Vol. 149). Palo Alto: Stanford University Press.
8. Chernoff, H. A., Kelly, C. M., & Kroger, J. R. (1996). The politics of crime. *Harvard Journal on Legislation, 33*, 527–579.
9. Davies, H. J. (2007). Understanding variations in murder clearance rates: The influence of the political environment. *Homicide Studies, 11*, 133–150
10. Bass, S. (2000). Negotiating change: Community organizations and the politics of policing. *Urban Affairs Review, 36*, 148–177.
11. Tunnell, K. D., & Gaines, L. K. (1992). Political pressures and influences on police executives: A descriptive analysis. *American Journal of Police, 1*, 1–16.
12. Iannone, N. F. (1987). *Supervision of police personnel* (4th ed., pp. 24–25). Upper Saddle River, NJ: Prentice Hall.
13. Schroeder, D. J., Lombardo, F., & Strollo, J. (1995). *Management and supervision of law enforcement* (pp. 34–35). Binghampton, NY: Gould Publications.
14. Adams, T. F. (2007). *Police field operations* (7th ed.). NJ: Prentice Hall.
15. Hale, C. (1981). *Police patrol: Operations and management*. NJ: Wiley.
16. International Association of Chiefs of Police (1977) The Patrol Operation. 3rd edn. (IACP).
17. Giacalone, J. (2011). *The criminal investigative function: A guide for new investigators*. NY: Looseleaf Law Publications.
18. Lyman, M. D. (2008). Criminal investigation: The art and the science. Upper Saddle River, NJ: Prentice Hall.
19. Sonne, W. J. (2006). *Criminal investigation for the professional investigator*. Boca Raton: CRC Press.
20. National Institute of Justice (2000). Crime scene investigation. National Institute of Justice, NCJ# 178280.
21. Swanson, C., Chemelin, N., & Territo, L. (1996). *Criminal investigation* (6th ed.). NY: McGraw-Hill.

22. Geberth, V. J. (1996). *Practical homicide investigation: Tactics, procedures and forensic techniques.* Boca Raton: CRC Press.
23. Hess, K. M, Orthmann, C. H. (2010). Criminal investigation (9th ed.). Clifton Park, NY: Delmar Cengage.
24. Wells, G. L. et al. (1998). Eyewitness identification procedures: Recommendations for lineups and photo spreads. *Law and Human Behavior 22,* 603, 615–616
25. Bailey, W. G. (Ed.). (1995). *The encyclopedia of police science* (2nd ed., Vol. 361). London: Routledge.
26. McDevitt, D. S. (2009). *Major case management: A guide for law enforcement managers.* Springfield: Charles C. Thomas.
27. Lehrer, J. (2012). When memory commits an injustice, April 14. The Wall Street Journal. C18
28. Morley, Patrick. (2008). *Report writing for criminal justice professionals.* New York: Kaplan Publishing.
29. Henning, P. J. et al. (2010). Mastering criminal procedure (Vol. 52). Durham, NC: Carolina Academic Press.
30. Duncan, K., Gruneberg, M., & Wallis, D. (Eds.). (1980). *Changes in working life.* New York: Wiley.
31. Reason, J. (1997). *Managing the risks of organizational accidents.* Aldershot: Ashgate.
32. Kock, R. (1999). *The 80–20 Principle: The secret to success by achieving more with less.* New York: Doubleday.
33. Bachman, R., & Paternoster, R. (2004). *Statistics for criminology and criminal justice.* New York: McGraw-Hill.

# Chapter 7
# Discussion, Policy Implications, Limitations and Directions for Future Research

## 7.1 Discussion

What can criminal justice learn from a single case study? This study revealed how a person can be misidentified during a police show-up, the failure points during the preliminary investigation that may have facilitated the misidentification and the failure points during the follow-up investigation that may have accelerated the harm (or failed to stop the harm sooner). The study also revealed proof of concept that the organizational accident framework is well suited for investigating critical police incidents. Approaching accidents through a systems theory of causation can help police managers, supervisors and support staff act with foresight and imagination to identify system failures *before* they occur leading to a safer work environment. Applying this theory of accidents to police work and replicating the study here can strengthen the theory so that across a range of critical incidents (e.g., use of force, vehicular pursuit, wrongful arrest), patterns of behavior and contributing factors reveal themselves to become predictable and, consequently, generalizable.

This case represents a "near miss"—to use aviation parlance—in criminal justice practice, insofar as the plaintiff was not convicted and sent to prison, but was clearly on that course. Had the plaintiff been convicted there would not have been any DNA to exonerate him since any potential trace evidence left behind on the weapon was never collected. The data revealed that police procedures designed to guard against such errors at the operating level were not followed and that omissions—failing to act—was a recurring theme that presented a greater risk than acts of commission. These errors were likely facilitated by latent conditions—training, supervision, management practices—that were left unchecked, or under developed. This single case should be sufficient for police managers to pause and examine those conditions to determine how they contribute to active failures at the operating level and to reduce uncertainty in the future when hazardous law enforcement procedures arise. Organizationally, this translates into the planning function involving people skillful enough to undertake strategic planning exercises and managers willing to support them as they attempt to uncover "trivial" and hidden assumptions that can be dangerous if unleashed.

J. Shane, *Learning from Error in Policing*, SpringerBriefs in Policing,
DOI: 10.1007/978-3-319-00041-1_7, © The Author(s) 2013

An organizational accident is in effect "the house that Jack built." When the accident does occur, it is a cumulative event that does not necessarily tell the story of Jack's house (the individual police agency), or of Jack who built the house (the police chief and command staff); rather, it shows how the house (the police agency) is indirectly linked to other things in the house (subculture, political climate, established policies, formal and informal operating practices) and the people connected to the house (front-line police officers, supervisors and top administrators) in the incident. The organizational accident methodology allows the account of "the man all tattered and torn" (the person so harmed) to be told as the circumstances (various acts and omissions) are unpacked showing how they are interrelated. Each stage of the event is an example of a nested subordinate organizational issue that signals an incremental descent into an active failure. The last phase of the event (unsafe act) is difficult to disentangle and does not have sufficient explanatory power for the losses if the previous stages are not present (refer to Fig. 2.1). It is not possible to divorce the unsafe act from the context in which it occurred and the organizational accident framework takes context into account. The appropriate inquiry then shifts from how did the individual fail the organization, to how did the organization fail the individual? When an accident occurs, police managers/supervisors share the risk and accountability with the individual who committed the unsafe act.

Working from the top of the organization downward the research revealed that a local policy on show-up identifications was not promulgated and management failed to detect its absence. Similarly, state- and County-level policies were silent on show-up procedures despite direction from the U.S. Supreme Court in 1972 and the wealth of social science and psychological research that has surfaced since then describing the problems associated with eyewitness identification and show-up procedures. This left the officers in the field to improvise without any operating guidelines and little or no way to moderate the competing interests of production and safety. Although some city officers did receive training in show-up procedures earlier in their career, periodic maintenance of those skills is not required and there is no record of recent training, which is a managerial flaw that widens the gap between production and safety. Because show-ups are a relatively uncommon police practice the officers' skills likely evanesced throughout time.

Although there is only indirect evidence of internal and external pressure for results, it is sufficient for management to look closer at operations and culture to determine whether informal practices, tacit messages and shortcuts are supplanting formal procedures in the interest of crime control. There is testimonial evidence that supports show-ups routinely occur in the City police department as depicted in this study. This implicates the supervisory chain, insofar as an accepted past practice had been established, which means managers and supervisors likely knew about the informal practice beforehand, they tolerated it and failed to correct it.

As a measure of organizational defense, supervision also failed. The on-scene supervisor in this case (a mid-level police manager) made both procedural decision errors and poor-choice errors, despite his previous training and experience supervising criminal investigations. The lieutenant conceded at deposition he did not know the correct procedures, but proceeded anyway, which may be why he also failed to issue specific instructions to his subordinates—he simply did not know what to tell them. This was compounded by the shoddy preliminary investigation, which failed to collect corroborating evidence and the lack of situational awareness about what the officers knew and when they knew it *before* the show-up was assembled; there was a wealth of information that suggested an investigative detention, not an arrest was the more prudent course of action.

The lack of situational awareness began when the 911 operator failed to elicit pertinent details from the caller who reported the robbery and when the original officer contacted the victim and failed to collect and transmit sufficient details about the crime. Both of these omissions resulted in lost opportunities to identify the offenders and collect evidence from witnesses. As the officers proceeded under ambiguous circumstances, they relied on perceptual shorthand to fill in the gaps instead of corroborated evidence from the witnesses. The documents revealed there was a wealth of disconfirming evidence regarding the plaintiff's involvement, yet the officers pressed forward. Ultimately, when the officers presented the victim to the alleged offenders in a simultaneous show-up, the last organizational safeguard was breached. This procedural error provoked the misidentification; then the officers acted on the victim's equivocal identification about the offenders' involvement; the arrest set the criminal justice apparatus in motion.

In the end, concern should not be about this given case; rather, it should be whether police leaders are willing to respond to the general propositions presented in this case with appropriate initiative that helps all police departments prevent similar future accidents (i.e., situational and organizational influences on personnel; training; systematic review of critical incidents). Senior-level law enforcement management should apply the findings of this case in the context of their given police agency; it is those who *receive* the information presented in this study that must determine whether and how the specifics of this case fit with their idiosyncratic situation. Granted we are dealing with hindsight—which is often 20/20—but it is hindsight that enables police policymakers to shape the future (through policy development and training), so warnings and indicators become more obvious the next time around. Each person in a police department—civilian and sworn—has a responsibility to act as a safety agent, but the lower levels take their cues from personnel upstream in the organization. Top police administrators must accept responsibility for risk, failure, success and safety by remaining conscientious about the results their decisions have on the system if they are to prevent future accidents.

## 7.2  Policy Implications

From a procedural perspective, police management must adopt written policies and review and revise existing policies on when police officers are allowed to perform a show-up in the field.[1] Although there are baseline procedural standards for conducting show-ups (e.g., *U.S. v. Wade,* 1967; *Neil v. Biggers,* 1972), as a matter of managerial prerogative, there is nothing restricting police agencies from adopting more stringent show-up standards under a narrower set of circumstances.[2] Individual police agencies need not wait for a judicial imperative via case law to compel them to adopt, or revise their policies. They should take the initiative to align their policies with findings from contemporary legal and scientific research governing eyewitness identification. Knowing the problems associated with eyewitness identification that have been uncovered through empirical research, there is no good reason to prolong the inevitable, nor continue assuming unnecessary risk when other methods are available.

Police management should also adopt a comprehensive error management program, whose primary goal is to reduce errors and shape a culture of safety. The program should include system-wide measures to (1) minimize active failures in the field; (2) minimize the risks associated with complex tasks such as show-up procedures; (3) uncover and evaluate errors and violations, particularly routine errors; and (4) implement measures to detect latent conditions.[3] Critical incident review is clearly concerned with why individuals do not do what they are supposed to do, but it is more concerned with the situational and organizational influences on the individual's behavior (i.e., latent conditions) and what to do about them.

Focusing on latent conditions and other organizational influences likely offers more promise of positive change than trying to change the person in the same way situational crime prevention offers more promise of controlling crime than changing individual social circumstances (i.e., poverty, unemployment, maternal deprivation). To do this, organizations must block opportunities for accidents to occur by erecting multi-layered defenses that are impervious to unintentional

---

[1]  *See* Ref. [1].

[2]  The best example of police agencies self-imposing higher standards for officer conduct is the use of deadly force. The constitutional baseline for police use of deadly force in the United States is Tn. v. Garner (471 U.S. 1, 1985), which commands police officers shall not apprehend unarmed, non-violent fleeing felons by using deadly force. Following the *Garner* decision, many police agencies self-imposed higher standards via administrative policy to prevent unnecessary shootings and firearms discharges, which led to significant decreases in police shootings nationwide (*see* [2–5]).

[3]  Reason 1997 [6] at 125; *see also* [7]; *see generally* Walker [8] at 100–134 (discussing data collection as part of an early warning system to improve officer performance); CAROL A. ARCHBOLD, MANAGING THE BOTTOM LINE: RISK MANAGEMENT IN POLICING (in [9]) (discussing risk management in American police agencies); JENS RASMUSSEN, WHAT CAN BE LEARNED FROM HUMAN ERROR REPORTS (in [10]); [11].

failures, insofar as possible. This requires an acculturation in that direction, which means managers and supervisors must express behaviors, attitudes, symbols and expectations that reflect trust and safety between them and line personnel[4]; positive and negative implicit messages from top administrators can affect officers' decisions without them realizing it.[5] Adopting this type of safety consciousness is already occurring in the fire service and should be adopted by the police service.[6]

The failure profile revealed that just a few categories of error represent a sizeable proportion of all failures. This suggests that police managers and supervisors should focus their attention specifically on organizational defenses aimed at those categories, which is more rational and efficient instead of negotiating solutions for individual officers time after time. Procedural omissions accounted for the largest error category, which means officers failed to take the correct course of action when needed, which created unnecessary risk. This may have occurred because the task was complex, the officers did not receive adequate and timely training and they did not have a readily available field reference. One practical, albeit imperfect, solution is to develop a field checklist for procedural guidance. While the show-up procedure is deceptively simple on its face, there are five steps that need to be undertaken to ensure due process. When each step is adhered to not only is the accused protected, but the police are also forearmed with factual information they can use to justify their decisions. A preformatted checklist grounded in procedural law leaves the officers with a systematic set of questions to ask, a permanent record for the court to examine regarding the out-of-court identification process and evidence of policy compliance should anyone inquire, such as police supervisors and prosecutors.[7]

Next, there is a gap in standardized critical incident review methodology, which means it is up 17,000± law enforcement agencies nationwide to do it themselves, each with a different approach. As such, all law enforcement agencies should adopt[8] the organizational accident framework as the national standard for evaluation. This will allow police agencies to systematically collect information about

---

[4] *See* Refs. [12–14].

[5] *See* Refs. [15, 16].

[6] Ted Putnam, *Findings From the Wildland Firefighters Human Factors Workshop: Improving Wildland Firefighter Performance Under Stressful, Risky Conditions: Toward Better Decisions on the Fireline and More Resilient Organizations,* (U.S. Forest Service June 1995).

[7] (For example, police agencies pursuing CALEA accreditation and re-accreditation must present evidence of policy compliance); *see also* Reason 2002 [11] at 40 (discussing how to reduce errors by omission through task analysis and reminders).

[8] The National Policing Improvement Agency (U.K.) is refining the organizational accident model for all British police forces; *see also* Charles Vincent, Sally Taylor-Adams & Nicola Stanhope, *Framework for Analysing Risk and Safety in Clinical Medicine,* 316 BMJ 1154 (1998) (where the medical community is moving more toward evidence-based practices with a focus on systematically collecting data to inform practice). CALEA could drive this effort in the United States together with leading police advocacy groups such as the Police Foundation; Police Executive Research Forum; National Sheriff's Association; International Association of Chief of Police and the National Institute of Justice.

the four interconnected factors that undergird most critical incidents. Data that are systematically collected can be categorized and statistically analyzed across a wide array of police agencies for recurring patterns and trends, for error-prone tasks and for the strengths and weaknesses in organizational defenses. The results of such a widespread data collection effort will inform police practice in the way the U.S. National Transportation Safety Board (NTSB) informs aviation safety and the U.S. Nuclear Regulatory Commission (NRC) informs nuclear power safety.

The U.S. Department of Justice (DOJ) should assume leadership in this vacuum by mandating,[9] cataloging and publishing after-action reports on organizational accidents on a national scale to improve police practice.[10] In this way, the DOJ would act in a manner similar to the Joint Commission (formerly the Joint Commission for the Accreditation of Healthcare Organizations), whose mission is to improve healthcare practice by collaborating with industry stakeholders to evaluate healthcare programs and practices with an eye toward providing safe and effective health care. One of the ways the Joint Commission fulfills its mission is by collecting and analyzing sentinel events; sentinel events are any unanticipated events that result in death, serious physical injury or psychological injury to a patient, which is not related to the patient's illness (e.g., iatrogenic harm or medical malpractice). By analyzing these events, patterns and trends can be uncovered toward improving performance and identifying root causes so adverse outcomes can be averted or at least mitigated. Action plans with specific tasks and deadlines typically follow the findings from a Join Commission review, and the Joint Commission usually links root cause analysis to a healthcare provider's

---

[9] To ensure compliance, the mandate must be tied to consequences. The federal government should, at a minimum, tie the mandate to federal funding such as police-related grants and withhold funding for failing to comply.

[10] Three notable examples of organizational accidents in policing that were never documented for the learning value include (1) in 2010 two Newark, NJ police detectives were indicted for official misconduct for allegedly showing a robbery victim a single photograph of an alleged offender instead of the required sequential photo display, which led to a biased identification in an effort to bolster their case. Two different judges dismissed the charges against the detectives and the alleged offender, see [17, 18]; (2) in 1999, the Los Angeles police department Rampart corruption scandal involved police officers stealing, selling narcotics and committing perjury to bolster cases against alleged gang members. The investigating panel noted "It appears that nobody had the desire or political will to complete the after-action report...," see Rampart Reconsidered at 62–63; and (3) in 1997, four men falsely confessed to the Norfolk, VA, police department to a crime that they did not commit. Infamously known as the "Norfolk Four," the lead homicide detective, Robert Glenn Ford, was subsequently convicted on two counts of extortion and one count of making false statements to the FBI and sentenced to federal prison. Previously, Ford allegedly extracted false confessions from teenagers involved in a crime, but the Norfolk police department did not produce an after-action report detailing the accident, see [19, 20, 21, 22, 23, 24, 25, 26, 27, 28]; PBS Frontline, *The Confessions* (documenting the trial of four men who falsely confessed to a murder in Norfolk, VA that they did not commit; the confessions were based largely on oppressive, yet legal police tactics that are tantamount to failure in a police organization, see [25]. Accessible at http://www.pbs.org/wgbh/pages/frontline/the-confessions, 2010) and http://www.norfolkfour.com, retrieved on December 22, 2012.

continued accreditation. There are potential obstacles to transferring this model to U.S. policing since the DOJ does not oversee, or regulate policing at any level and does not mandate police agency accreditation; therefore, imposing sentinel event reporting requirements is not necessarily tied to any consequences and would be voluntary.

If evidence-based practices are believed to be best to inform public policy and professional practice, then empirical evidence from systematic accident review has many benefits such as discontinuing outmoded or harmful practices, improving police officers' knowledge, skills and abilities and providing a framework for training and education. This is an important step forward for a progressive society, particularly for policing as it continues to advance through training, management and policy development.

Lastly, the police must incorporate more training. The record in this case shows that police received some minimal training in show-ups, but did not receive regular updated legal training; indeed, such training is discretionary and is not mandated by the city or the state. Training that is scenario based and interactive with immediate feedback, which is rooted in relevant cognitive data can help police officers develop better situational awareness and decision-making skills by giving them an opportunity to apply what they have learned to a realistic situation. A culture of safety should include training on police policy and procedure imbued with organizational culture, managerial expectations, ethics, situational context, empathy, civics and contemporary legal procedure. This will provide officers with greater perspective on who they are dealing with, alternative explanations for behavior and the implications for their decisions. This also helps shape the officers' perceptions, interpretations and motivations and triggers a sense of caution, which may lead to more consistent, objectively verifiable and reasoned decisions.[11]

Taken together the policy implications mean policing must demand better from itself. This means foregoing a dismissive attitude toward organizational accidents as nothing more than sharp criticism and an opportunity to "beat up" on the police in favor of embracing them as a teaching tool intended to prevent harm to police officers and citizens alike. It also means shrugging off complacency and banality to treat comfort zones as danger zones simply because an accident has not occurred; reacting to accidents with investigative vigor, not necessarily to lay blame but to improve professional practice; proactively constructing scenarios and "war gaming" (i.e., playing devil's advocate) them through the planning process, where policies and practices are "red teamed" (i.e., independently evaluated to challenge the organization to improve effectiveness) for strengths and weaknesses; and partnering with research universities and leading police advocacy groups to assist with these activities in the name of evaluation research and education to defend against similar consequences.

---

[11] *See* Ref. [29]; Mauboussin Michael J. Mauboussin, Think twice: the power of counter intuition at 120–136 (2009) (discussing empathy and the implications for better decisions).

## 7.3 Limitations

We must be mindful this research is an early effort to apply a theory of organizational accidents to a show-up procedure, and while it does provide a glimpse into police practice, there are some limitations. First, the results are from a single case of a single type of error. There is no U.S. or international data collection standard for show-up identifications. Therefore, it is not possible to establish baseline measures to uncover trends and patterns from which to estimate show-up errors and to determine if this case is a statistical departure from "the norm." This limits the study's strength of external validity, to a degree. However, the subjective experiences of the actors are important and offer utility for identifying and closing the gaps in organizational failure across the wider law enforcement community and these experiences coupled with the functional analysis of the case itself produces intimate, practical and context-dependent knowledge, which is essential for learning from error and developing personal mastery.[12] It is the rich contextual attributes that increase the inferential possibilities of this single case study.

Second, the content coding was subjective and was not subjected to inter-rater reliability. This may introduce bias based on subjective interpretations, which is partly the criticism of qualitative research designs in general. The GFT classification scheme developed by James Reason (Table 3.2) contains some ambiguity, which affects mutual exclusivity and, thus, validity. Also, determining who is responsible for a given error (agency role) is not without its idiosyncrasies; for example, when a supervisor and line-level officer are present and an error occurs, both the line officer and the supervisor may share responsibility for the error, which also affects mutual exclusivity. Similarly, exactly when a preliminary investigation ends and when a follow-up investigation begins varies and is not necessarily precise, which may affect the number of tasks associated with each investigative stage. Any initial coding errors may also affect where the failures are situated according to the four aspects of organizational failure (Fig. 2.1). Although the observed failures fit reasonably well with Reason's GFT categories, there is room for improvement and future research should explore re-conceptualizing failure categories that are germane to policing.

Third, a complete understanding of why omissions predominate, why certain decisions occurred and whether those decisions were intentional or unintentional is not known. This work explored *how* omissions occurred and that they presented the greatest risk, but we do not know exactly *why* they occurred and what influenced them beyond some speculation (e.g., lack of policy, lack of timely in-service

---

[12] *See* Refs. [30, 31]; (to develop personal mastery in police executives, the Senior Management Institute for Police—an intensive management training course for senior police executives—hosted by Harvard University's John F. Kennedy School of Government and the Police Executive Research Forum uses the case study method of instruction with cases derived from corporate, public and police agencies, *see* http://www.policeforum.org/about-us/perf-departments/smip.dot accessed December 29, 2012).

training, laziness, mental fatigue, memory lapse, medical condition). Similarly, we do not know why certain decisions were perceived as good choices by the decision-makers at the moment. For example, the analysis revealed that probable cause to arrest did not exist; however, the police officers perceived that it did exist. Why did the supporting detective on scene fail to notify the show-up administrator (the lieutenant) about her observations regarding the victim's equivocal identification during the show-up (e.g., fear of group ostracism; deficiencies in her own technical or legal acumen)? If she knew the victim was not certain because he doubted one of the offenders' identities, then she knew probable cause did not exist for his arrest; if probable cause did not exist, then the arrest was unlawful and should not have occurred, yet it did.

Fourth, there is a lack of comparison. This case is not compared to a successful police show-up, so we do not know how aspects of a procedurally correct show-up might compare. The lack of comparison leaves us with a one-sided picture only able to see the errors, but not what worked under similar circumstances. Are most show-ups conducted in this manner? Could a show-up conducted in this manner still capture the true offender? What are the differences between successful and unsuccessful show-ups?

Fifth, the research relies on data contained within the source documents, which were not prepared for research purposes. There was no opportunity to re-interview the victim, the offenders or the witnesses to clarify details or collect more data, nor an opportunity to interview top police administrators and delve deeper into the organization's culture and structure. There may have been conflicting priorities of budgeting, efficiency and safety, where due process lost out to crime control and training was sacrificed in the interest of a fiscally leaner operation. This may have contributed to a legalistic/"lock 'em up" policing style. While the source documents did provide good insight into police practice, they did not provide any medical, psychological, pharmacological, cultural or organizational data.

Lastly, although the organizational accident framework holds some promise for setting an investigative standard for critical incidents, the model is not granular. The model is sufficient for uncovering high-level qualitative details about the accident, but it cannot determine micro-level quantitative details about a given accident (e.g., how many more officers or supervisors do we need to ensure safety? How much more should the budget increase to ensure safety? How much training do we need?). These are value judgments that limit the impact of science.

## 7.4 Directions for Future Research

Future research should focus on developing a larger pool of out-of-court identifications that includes show-ups, line-ups and photographic displays across a diverse population of victims, witnesses, offenders and types of crimes to assess risk. A larger and more diverse pool of subjects will likely reveal different risks for different crimes and different identification processes. Repeated accidents involving different people and different incidents with similar outcomes may implicate causal factors relating to the workplace and the operating system, not necessarily the employee. Research suggests that eyewitness identification does suffer from problems[13] and the Innocence Project claims that 75% of wrongful convictions involve eyewitness misidentification.[14] If, as the Innocence Project asserts, that "…wrongful convictions are not isolated or rare events but instead arise from systemic defects," then identifying the risks of various identification procedures and devising suitable safeguards provides a measure of safety.[15] This research offers a small window into where some of those defects may reside and how to correct them.

Future research should also focus on the psychological implications of groupthink and how groupthink may correlate with field enforcement practices. Groupthink is "a mode of thinking people engage in when they are deeply involved in a cohesive in-group, when the members' striving for unanimity override their motivation to realistically appraise alternative courses of action…a deterioration of mental efficiency, reality testing and moral judgment that results from in-group pressures."[16] The major hypothesis behind the theory is that groups that display groupthink symptoms are more likely to produce poor decision outcomes.

Policing bears many groupthink attributes including structural faults of the organization (e.g., insular culture; homogeneity of members—social background and ideology; traditional lack of impartial leadership; loyalty toward the organization over loyalty to the profession), provocative situational context (e.g., high external stress; highly consequential decisions; pressure due to time constraints), pressure toward uniformity (e.g., direct pressure on dissenters; illusion of unanimity), overestimation of the group (e.g., feelings of invulnerability) and closed mindedness (e.g., stereotyping out-groups; collective rationalizations). From these antecedents flow the symptoms of poor decisions such as an incomplete survey of alternatives, failure to examine the risks of the preferred course of action and poor information search.[17] Some of these attributes appear to be present in this case, and it is important to know how and why they contribute to wrongful arrests.

---

[13] *See* Steblay, Dysert, Fulero & Lindsay [25].

[14] *See* http://www.innocenceproject.org/Content/What_are_the_causes_of_wrongful_convictions. php. Accessed March 8, 2012.

[15] Some safety measures are already in place such as double blind and sequential, not simultaneous, photographic identification procedures.

[16] *See* Refs. [32]; *see also* [33–36]; Michael J. Mauboussin, Think twice: the power of counter intuition at 18 (2009) (discussing the issues of tunnel vision); [37].

[17] *See* Ref. [38], see references Souryal & Mckay [39] and Souryal [40]; Mauboussin Michael J. Mauboussin, Think twice: the power of counter intuition at 71–72 (2009) (cautioning against the "institutional imperative" of blind loyalty to one's peers); [41] (describing his now famous "obedience experiment" that uncovered peoples' ease and willingness to obey orders from authority figures even when they know the orders are likely to be painful or immoral regardless of the potential adverse consequences. In policing, officers are inclined to conform to their superiors' orders rather than speak up even when they know something is wrong for fear of being labeled disobedient and brought up on administrative charges for obedience to orders or

To understand why certain decisions were made it is necessary to know how police officers learn to make decisions, what they are taught about decision making and what informs their decisions (e.g., ethics, rule of law, policies, subculture, organizational climate).[18] Errors may result from a trade-off between the appeal of the short-term gratification (e.g., a sense of public safety through immediate arrest; public respect; career success; practicality)[19] and the long-term gratification whose appeal is attenuated by time, distance and procedure (e.g., methodical evidence collection and a slow judicial process resulting in arrest and conviction). In the latter instance, internal and external pressure for results (i.e., production pressures favoring arrest) implicates time and efficiency such that to forego the immediate arrest means a lengthier more costly investigation that encumbers personnel and extends the time to case closure, which may have negative political ramifications. The arena where law enforcement activity is carried out is imbued with individual zeal and the competitive game of pursuit (officers) and evasion (criminals) is one where ferreting out criminal behavior is a constant test of ingenuity and determination. In the interest of pleasing management and saving face before a cunning criminal, individual officers are likely to err on the side of the organization (i.e., crime control) instead of the alleged criminal (i.e., due process), which may have contributed to the haste in this case.

It would also be interesting to know how incidents such as this (wrongful arrest) affect police-community relations and police legitimacy. Being unlawfully arrested and held in jail for several months is likely to generate a great deal of long-lasting negative resentment. Vicarious experience (i.e., indirect police contact through family and friends) is also likely to negatively affect attitude and sentiment toward the police in general.

Lastly, do police departments that are nationally accredited through CALEA suffer more, less or the same errors in their practices as those that are not accredited? CALEA touts two benefits of accreditation as "greater accountability within the agency" and "reduced risk and liability exposure."[20] If CALEA's claims are accurate, then law enforcement accreditation may contribute to reducing organizational accidents.

---

(Footnote 17 continued)

insubordination. When the show-up was improperly assembled by the lieutenant, although the officers knew—or may have known—it was improper, they were not inclined to question their superior's decision).

[18] For example, police forces in the U.K. have uniformly adopted the "national decision model," developed by the National Police Improvement Agency, which is intended to improve decision making. The model is built on five principles that surround the mission and core values of all U.K. police services: (1) identify the situation and gather more information; (2) assess threats and risks of the situation; (3) consider powers, policies and other obligations; (4) identify options and consider possible contingencies; and (5) take appropriate action and review what happened. Decisions can be measured against this rubric to determine their strengths and weaknesses; *see also* [42, 43].

[19] *See* Ref. [44].

[20] *See* http://www.calea.org/content/law-enforcement-program-benefits. Accessed March 19, 2012.

# References

1. Cicchini, M. D., & Easton, J. G. (2010). Reforming the law on show-up identifications. *Journal of Criminal Law and Criminology, 100*, 101–133.
2. Skolnick, J. H., & Fyfe, J. J. (1993). *Above the law: Police use of excessive force*. New York: The Free Press.
3. Fyfe, J. J. (1988). Police use of deadly force: Research and reform. *Justice Quarterly, 5*, 165–206.
4. Tannenbaum, A. N. (1994). The influence of the garner decision on police use of deadly force. *Journal of Criminal Law and Criminology, 85*, 241.
5. Geller, W. A., & Scott, M. S. (1992). *Deadly force: What we know: A practitioner's desk reference on police-involved shootings* (pp. 267–275). Police executive research forum.
6. Reason, J. (1997). *Managing the risks of organizational accidents*. Aldershot: Ashgate.
7. Meurier, C. E. (2000). Understanding the nature of errors in nursing: using a model to analyse critical incident reports of errors which had resulted in an adverse or potentially adverse event. *Journal of Advanced Nursing, 32*, 202–207.
8. Walker, S. (2005). *The New World of Police Accountability*. (pp. 46–49). Thousand Oaks, CA: Sage
9. Archbold, C. A. (2013). *Policing* (pp. 341–355). Beverley Hills: Sage.
10. Duncan, K., Gruenberg, M., & Wallis, D. (Eds.). (1980). *Changes in working life*. New York: Wiley.
11. Reason, J. (2002). Combating omission errors through task analysis and good reminders. *Quality and Safety in Health Care, 11*, 40–44.
12. Zohar, D. (1980). Safety climate in industrial organizations: Theoretical and applied implications. *Journal of Applied Psychology, 65*, 96–102.
13. Dunbar, R. (1975). Manager's influence on subordinates' thinking about safety. *The Academy of Management Journal, 18*, 364–369.
14. Gunningham, N., & Sinclair, D. (2009). Organizational trust and the limits of management-based regulation. *Law and Society Review, 43*, 865–900.
15. Douglas, M. (1987). *How institutions think*. London: Routledge & Kegan Paul.
16. Burawoy, M. (1979). *Manufacturing consent*. Chicago: University of Chicago Press.
17. Friedman, A. (2010). Trial set to begin for newark police officers charged with misconduct. The Star Ledger, April 20.
18. Friedman, A. (2011). Misconduct charges against newark officer are dropped. The Star Ledger, February 2.
19. Scheck, B., Neufeld, P., & Dwyer, J. (2000). *Actual innocence: Five days to execution and other dispatches from the wrongly convicted* (Vol. 264). New York: Random House.
20. Garrett, B. (2011). *Convicting the innocent: Where criminal prosecutions go wrong*. Cambridge: Harvard University Press.
21. Ede, R., & Shephard, E. (2000). *Active defense*. London: Law Society Publishing.
22. Leo, R. a. (2008). *Police interrogation and American justice*. Cambridge: Harvard University Press.
23. Kassin, S., Drizin, S., Grisso, T., Gudjonsson, G., Leo, R., & Redlich, A. (2010). police-induced confessions: Risk factors and recommendations. *Law and Human Behavior, 34*, 3–38.
24. Gould, J. B., & Leo, R. A. (2010). One hundred years of getting it wrong: Wrongful convictions after a century of research. *Journal of Criminal Law and Criminology, 100*, 825–868.
25. Steblay, N., Dysert, J., Fulero, S., & Lindsay, R. C. L. (2001). Eyewitness accuracy rates in police show-up and line-up presentations: A meta-analytic comparison. *Law and Human Behavior, 27*, 523–540.
26. Yarmey, D. A., Yarmey, M. J., & Yarmey, L. A. (1996). Accuracy of eyewitness identifications in showups and lineups. *Law and Human Behavior, 20*, 459–477.

27. Connors, E., Lundregan, T., Miller, N., & Mcewan, T. (1996). *Convicted by Juries, exonerated by science: Case studies in the use of DNA evidence to establish innocence after trial.* Washington, D.C.: National Institute of Justice.

28. Hara, P. O'. (2005). *Why law enforcement organizations fail: Mapping the organizational fault lines in policing, at 15.* Durham, NC: Carolina Academic Press.

29. Kunda, Z. (1990). The case for motivated reasoning. *Psychological Bulletin, 108,* 480–498.

30. Flyvberg, B. (2006). Five misunderstandings about case-study research. *Qualitative Inquiry, 12*(2), 219–245.

31. Kennedy, M. M. (1979). Generalizing from single case studies. *Evaluation Review, 3*(4), 661–678.

32. Janis, I. L. (1972). *Victims of groupthink* (p. 9). Boston: Houghton Mifflin Co.

33. Janis, I. (1983) Groupthink: psychological studies of policy decisions and fiascoes (2nd rev. ed.). Boston: Houghton Mifflin.

34. Moorhead, G., Ference, R., & Neck, C. P. (1991). Group decision fiascoes continue: space shuttle challenger and a revised groupthink framework. *Human Relations, 44,* 539–550.

35. Hart, P. T. (1990). *Groupthink in government: A study of small groups and policy failure.* Amsterdam: Swets & Zeitlinger.

36. Findley, K., & Scott, M. (2006). The multiple dimensions of tunnel vision in criminal cases. *Wisconsin Law Review, 291,* 291–397.

37. Bandes, S. (2006). Loyalty to one's convictions: The prosecutor and tunnel vision. *Howard Law Journal, 49,* 475–494.

38. Neck, C. P., & Moorhead, G. (1995). Groupthink remodeled: the importance of leadership, time pressure, and methodical decision-making procedures. *Human Relations, 48,* 546.

39. Souryal, S. S., & Mckay, B. W. (1996). Personal Loyalty to Superiors in Public Service. *Criminal Justice Ethics, 15,* 44–62.

40. Souryal S. S. (1999). Personal loyalty to superiors in criminal justice agencies. *Justice Quarterly, 16*(4), 871–895.

41. Milgram, S. (1963). Behavioural study of obedience. *Journal of Abnormal and Social Psychology, 67*(4), 371–378.

42. Thomas, K. T., & Walker, A. D. (2010). The sharp end: real life challenges in a complex activity space. *Journal of Public Affairs, 10,* 186–199.

43. Sinclair, H., Doyle, E. E. H., Johnston, D. M., & Paton, D. (2012). Decision-making training in local government emergency management. *International Journal of Emergency Management, 1,* 159–174.

44. Bayley, D. H. (2002). Law enforcement and the rule of law: Is there a tradeoff? *Criminology & Public Policy, 2,* 133–154.

.

# Chapter 8
# Conclusion

Adopting an organizational accident framework offers a measure of coherence, even if to a modest degree, to the fragmented, decentralized and disparate world that is American law enforcement. American law enforcement is unique among the Western world's policing practices, insofar as there is no centralized government authority regulating the police, law enforcement services are not integrated, and training, recruiting and lateral transfer are not uniform across the country. The organizational accident model presents a standard method to examine and learn from mistakes, so repeating the same mistake is lessened; said differently, it presents a unified structure for routinely learning from error. When systematic information about an accident is not collected and compared against a given standard (i.e., measured), it is not possible to state with any certainty how the agency plans to improve operations, or reduce risk. Blaming individual police officers for errors is not the answer for a sustained solution, inasmuch as individual officers are not the only stakeholders in the criminal justice system; police managers, prosecutors, public defenders, defense attorneys and judges all have an interest at stake and to ignore their contribution to the error is to remain in precarious territory.

The police are the largest, most visible segment of the criminal justice system. They will likely continue to bear the brunt of social criticism for errors that lead to grave consequences, particularly if it is later discovered that it was their initial conduct that facilitated the adverse outcome (i.e., wrongful arrest, wrongful conviction, homicide by misadventure). Therefore, it is they who have the most to gain by leading the charge to adopt a preventative system like the one discussed here. The implications are many, from the practical to the abstract (e.g., legitimacy), but one point is certain: unless and until the police embrace a systems approach to addressing errors, complex police organizations and the officers that reify them are destined to repeat them.

J. Shane, *Learning from Error in Policing*, SpringerBriefs in Policing,
DOI: 10.1007/978-3-319-00041-1_8, © The Author(s) 2013

# Afterword

By now, readers will have recognized that it is a mistake to take the title of Jon Shane's "Learning From Error in Policing: A Case Study in Organizational Accident Theory" too literally. This monograph delivers much more than the modest recounting of events that its title implies. Among its many virtues is the precision with which it mobilizes a mode of analysis that is currently unfamiliar to the criminal justice world but that both street-level practitioners and academic researchers will recognize immediately as one that blazes a promising new road forward.

The criminal justice system has coasted for a long time on the illusion of practical infallibility. Practitioners knew that this was a fiction, of course, but on balance, it seemed to be a fiction worth sustaining. Are there people in prison who said they are innocent? The response, "They all *say* they are innocent" was good enough to dispose of that worry—until the DNA exoneration cases began to roll in. Now, in the aftermath of the DNA cases, the public knows that criminal justice is no more immune to human error than is medicine, aviation, or industry, and the fundamental legitimacy of the system—its ability to generate public trust in the law—will depend to a high degree on how practitioners and policy-makers confront their own errors.

One way to react to this situation—the prevalent way—is to convene a blue ribbon Innocence Commission or Wrongful Conviction Task force. These groups of dignitaries distill "causes" from the exoneration lists, rank those causes by the frequency of their recurrence, and develop a reform agenda. In these schemes, cases are reduced to "an eyewitness case" or "a false confession case" or "a forensic error case" and the archetypes generated in this way are subjected to statistical analysis. Often "best practices" are identified, and sometimes those are embedded in rules, legislation, or checklists.

This strategy undoubtedly improves the odds. But no checklist can cover every eventuality, and from the moment it is instituted every new checklist or set of best practices is under immediate and aggressive assault from its environment—from economic pressures, rising crime rates, tightening budgets, and pressing clearance rate demands.

Shane is willing to accept the reality that there is no single cause for most mistakes, no "silver bullet" solution for most problems, and no permanent, stable "solution" for anything. His monograph shows how important it is to admit that nothing is simple: that every error is embedded in a complex event involving multiple actors, who make small choices that interact with each other and with latent system weaknesses.

Unexpectedly, this insight turns out to be liberating. Once we face the complexities of adverse events we can see that our challenge is not the ultimately hopeless one of protecting a presumptively reliable system from careless or incompetent humans; rather, it is to invigorate and continually improve system reliability by taking account of the inevitability of human error.

In Shane's hands, an error becomes not something to sweep under the rug, but a "sentinel event," a valuable lens through which we can learn important lessons about preventing future mistakes. We can give the good guys in the system something to do besides trying to catch and exorcise the lazy, incompetent, corrupt, bad guys.

Shane shows how even an apparently routine street show-up, can yield important lessons when treated as an "organizational accident". To do this, he clears away a substantial pile of dead wood. He concentrates on professionalism and reliability as criteria; not on the criterion of legality that the Warren Court's constitutional decisions have imposed on show-up and street stop performance. He assumes that no single-cause, "bad apple" explanation will explain everything. He recognizes that the fact that a street-level investigator or mid-level manager zigged when he should have zagged is often apparent only in hindsight, and that the real question if we want to prevent recurrences is why the wrong decision looked like the *right* decision at the time. He gives one small, retail policing event the sustained analytic attention it deserves, and by doing this he shows that this mundane "near miss" is important *because* of its mundane, retail nature—because of the number of times its scenario will be replayed if we don't intervene.

On the surface there is an element here of taking policing away from the lawyers and giving it back to the police. There's value in that, but there is more here than a call for reasserting police responsibility for police work. This study shows how the best of social science (here, the science of eyewitness memory), the best of process analysis and expertise, and most perceptive understanding of the gritty, thickly-textured nature of sharp-end decision-making can be brought into harness together. A reader can learn more about how and why an eyewitness case can go wrong from this monograph than from any other single source. And a reader can learn how the *next* eyewitness case will go wrong unless the lessons of this sentinel event are learned.

But those specific insights into eyewitness cases are not the most important aspect of this work. Shane's monograph also points to the possibility of a common ground on which all of the criminal system's stakeholders could—like their precursors in aviation, industry and medicine—meet, apply his "organizational accident" approach, and begin the work of continually improving system reliability.

I expect that readers will finish this "case history" eager to analyze the history of another case. Then another. And share the results. This is an important step—no make that leap—in the right direction.

—James Doyle

James Doyle, a Boston-based attorney, is the 2012–2013 Visiting Fellow at the U.S. National Institute of Justice, where he has explored mobilizing the lessons of Sentinel Events in improving criminal justice system reliability. He is the immediate past director of the Center for Modern Forensic Practice at John Jay College of Criminal Justice and is author of *True Witness: Cops, Courts, Science and the Battle Against Misidentification* (Palgrave 2005) and several articles on criminal justice error, including "Learning From Error In American Criminal Justice" (Journal of Criminal Law and Criminology 2010).

# Index

J. Shane, *Learning from Error in Policing*, SpringerBriefs in Policing,
DOI: 10.1007/978-3-319-00041-1, © The Author(s) 2013